Go for the Goal

Go for the Goal

A Champion's Guide to Winning in Soccer and Life

MIA HAMM

With Aaron Heifetz

Quill

An Imprint of HarperCollinsPublishers

If you experience any sustained pain or discomfort when trying the exercises and drills outlined in this book, stop, walk to the sidelines, and consult with your coach, parents, or, better yet, your physician before continuing. If you attempt to play with an injury, you risk a lot more than winning or losing a soccer match. Don't do it.

Photography credits are on page 255.

The use of Olympic Games images is authorized by the U.S. Olympic Committee.

A hardcover edition of this book was published in 1999 by Harper-Collins Publishers Inc.

First Quill edition published 2000.

Designed by Elliott Beard

The Library of Congress has catalogued the hardcover edition as follows:
Hamm, Mia.
    Go for the goal : a champion's guide to winning in soccer and life / Mia Hamm. — 1st ed.
        p.   cm.
    ISBN 0-06-019342-5
    1. Hamm, Mia.   2. Soccer—Training.   3. Soccer—Psychological aspects.   4. Success.   I. Heifetz, Aaron.   II. Title.
GV943.9.T7H35   1999
796.334'2—dc21   99-19592

ISBN 0-06-093159-0 (pbk.)

02 03 04 ❖/RRD 10 9 8 7 6 5 4 3

To my nephew Dillon.
Through all of the sorrow, we found joy.
I love you, buddy!

"The vision of a champion is someone who is bent over, drenched in sweat, at the point of exhaustion when no one else is watching."

—ANSON DORRANCE,
*head women's soccer coach,
University of North Carolina*

Contents

Acknowledgments   xi

Foreword   xiii

PART ONE
The Game Within the Game

1 No "Me" in Mia   3

2 Love the Game   15

3 Love the Ball   25

4 The Mental Game   31

5 The Physical Game   47

PART TWO
On the Field

6 Trapping: The Ball Is Your Servant   61

7 Passing:
Making Your Teammates Look Good   81

8 Dribbling: Take on Your Opponent   107

9 Shooting: Be a Finisher   136

10 Heading: Soccer's Own Skill   160

11 Goalkeeping:
The Last Line of Defense   178

PART THREE
The Complete Player

12 Consistency   189

13 Being a Winner   195

14 Champion of the World   202

Afterword: Winning It All   213

Talk the Talk: A Soccer Glossary   245

Acknowledgments

Like everything else in my life where I have achieved a measure of success, this book is the product of a team effort from start to finish. My name may be on the cover but I would like to credit the following people with assists: To my husband Christiaan for his unconditional support on and off the field; to my family and friends who will always be "my first team," I love you all; to my coaches (Anson, April, Colleen, Dino, Jay, Tony, and Lauren) and teammates for helping me not only become a better player but also a better person; to my agent David Bober for his never-ending good advice and friendship, you are the man!; to Aaron Heifetz, for his patience, enthusiasm and hard work on this project; to my editors at HarperCollins, David Hirshey and Jay Papasan, for believing in women's soccer and making this book be the best it could be.

I am grateful to the Southern California Blues Soccer Club who traveled three hours and stood around for another three to help with the photo shoot, and to Paul Murphy and Dean Stoyer at Nike for generously supplying equipment.

Finally, I owe a huge debt to the fans of the U.S. Women's Soccer team—the parents, the coaches, the players, and of course, the girls who scream for us at every game. We play for you.

Foreword

Soccer has been a part of my life for as long as I can remember. It has helped me grow as an athlete and as a person. I've made lifelong friends, learned to embrace competition, and gained self-confidence, all the while having a ball. I feel like I'm the luckiest woman in the world.

Playing for the U.S. Women's national team, winning the World Cup in '91 and earning an Olympic gold medal in '96 are great achievements in and of themselves but truly it was always my love of the game, not the trophies or accolades, that kept me going for the goal. If there is one thing that I would want readers to take away from this book, it's that the *fun*—the pure joy of kicking a ball on a soccer field, the time spent bonding with teammates and the feeling of being as fit and strong as you can be—is more important than any result. As you learn more about my life in these pages, I hope you will be as inspired by my passion for the sport as by my accomplishments on the field.

PART I

The Game Within the Game

ONE

No "Me" in Mia

My name is Mariel Margaret Hamm, but everyone calls me Mia. Many people say I'm the best women's soccer player in the world. I don't think so. And because of that, someday I just might be.

All my life I've been playing up, meaning I've challenged myself by competing with players older, bigger, more skillful, more experienced—in short, better than me. When I was six, my big brother, Garrett, ran circles around me. At ten, I joined an eleven-year-old-boys' team and, eventually, led them in scoring. Seven years later I found myself playing for the number-one college team in America after becoming the youngest player ever to suit up for the U.S. Women's National Team.

Was I that good? No, but early on coaches detected a competitive fire in me and fed it by continually pitting me against superior opponents. Back then I wasn't sure I fit in; after all, I was shy and a bit intimidated by players I had idolized. But each day I attempted to play up to their level and earn their respect, and I was improving faster than I had ever dreamed possible.

Me at age 11. Who knew one of the Sidewinders would end up winning an Olympic gold medal?

Now, with the National Team, I'm training and playing with some of the best players in the world every day. When I see their amazing skills and talents, I have no doubt that I still have a lot of work to do. Until I can head the ball with the authority of Tisha Venturini, pass with the touch and imagination of Kristine Lilly, shoot with the thunder of Michelle Akers, and command a team with the grit of Carla Overbeck and the wit of Julie Foudy, I'll keep striving to become the complete player. My teammates are the driving forces that push me to improve.

It is the responsibility of your teammates to nurture you through competition. Their intensity and determination set the tone of your training environment, the crucible in which you as a soccer player are formed. Do these players create an atmosphere that will help me improve? Do I push them every day? Do the coaches push us? Everyone plays a unique role in building a team that reaches for excellence.

On the National Team—and we dare to be great, whether it's a one-on-one drill, an intrasquad scrimmage, or a grudge match against Norway—everyone wants to win. We live for situations that challenge us, because to the woman, we want to drive ourselves to the limit and beyond.

On the first day of a training camp, we have a one-on-one tournament where we put our cards on the table. It's forwards going against forwards, midfielders clashing with midfielders, and defenders trying to prove who is the toughest of them all. We play three 2-minute games, but in that 6 minutes we play the most intense soccer you'll see in a training session anywhere.

Players are battling for loose balls, sliding to block shots, and doing anything within the rules and a few things that are questionable (I've got torn jerseys to prove it) to gain the upper hand. We do this because we all know we have to push one another all the time to win. If one person slacks off and doesn't give the maximum, she has shortchanged not just herself but also the person she is squared up against and the whole team.

Soccer is not an individual sport. I don't score all the goals, and the ones I do score are usually the product of a team effort. I don't keep the ball out of the back of the net on the other end of the field. I don't plan our game tactics. I don't wash our training gear (okay, sometimes I do), and I don't make our airline reservations. I am a member of a team, and

I rely on the team, I defer to it and sacrifice for it, because the team, not the individual, is the ultimate champion.

Once you experience success—and you will if you put in the work—you shouldn't be afraid to celebrate it. Unless you feel good about what you do every day, you won't do it with much conviction or passion. So celebrate what you've accomplished, but also raise the bar a little higher each time you succeed. I think that's what we do so well on the National Team. We've been successful, and we do enjoy being the best. But after the 1996 Olympics, once we got back together, all we talked about was reclaiming the World Cup. We never lost our focus on our next goal as we all used our success in '96 as motivation to win in '99.

Never let yourself get too comfortable or confident, because that's when a weaker opponent can sneak up and knock you off your perch. Take your victories, whatever they may be, cherish them, use them, but don't settle for them. There are always new, grander challenges to confront, and a true winner will embrace each one.

I firmly believe that success breeds success. Once you have achieved something, your confidence begins to build. You realize you're capable of doing it again. But each time you must work harder, because the old saying is true, it is more difficult to stay on top than to get there.

The U.S. Women's National Team got to stand on that gold medal podium not only because we beat China in the championship game but because of everything we did as a team in the years leading up to that moment. There were tremendous sacrifices made since the veteran core of National Team players first pulled on the U.S. jersey. We put families on hold, lost jobs because of the travel, and spent time away from friends. But as April Heinrichs, our captain at the 1991 Women's World Cup, used to say, it is not sacrifice if you love what you're doing.

I believe that to fit into a team, no individual can put her needs above those of the team as a whole. She must play her role, the position the coach assigns her. On the Olympic team, we had players who could've started but didn't complain when they were asked to contribute from the bench. They understood their role within the system. When they got into the game, they made the most of the opportunity.

Two shining examples of this are Shannon MacMillan and Tiffany Roberts. Eight months before the Olympics, Shannon was not even on the team, a victim of one of the final cuts when the coaches chose the roster for residency training camp. Shannon got a second chance and battled her way back into camp. She then earned a spot in the starting lineup and scored two goals en route to the Olympic semifinal.

Tiffany Roberts, a starter on the 1995 Women's World Cup team, found herself on the bench as a reserve because Shannon emerged in the months leading up to the Olympics. In the semifinal against Norway, our coaching staff decided we needed a tenacious and tough defender in the midfield to shut down Norway's brilliant center-midfielder, Hege Riise. Tiffany got the nod to start in place of Shannon, who became a reserve for the match. Not only did Tiffany play a great game, executing her role perfectly, but Shannon came off the bench to score the winning goal in sudden death overtime. I know it sounds almost unbelievable in this age of prima donna athletes, but I never heard either of them complain. There was no sniping or backbiting. And when they got on the field, both came through for us in a way that sealed their place in history.

Remember that in soccer, no role is set in stone. A coach may ask you to play a different position or come off the bench for only a game or one tournament. Roles can change every game, either in very small ways or dramatically. Maybe you're a forward, and one of your defenders gets hurt and suddenly you have to play defense for the rest of the year. You have to do what's best for the team. Maybe it will turn out to be a better position for you. In any case, take it as a compliment. Your coach felt that you were versatile enough to play more than one position, a talent that can come in handy. Often when a coach is forced to choose between two equally skillful players, she'll choose the more versatile of the two because it gives her more coaching options down the line.

Heading into the 1991 Women's World Cup, I was a reserve forward behind April Heinrichs, Michelle Akers, and Carin Gabarra. But before the tournament, one of our starting defenders, Megan McCarthy, suffered a severe knee injury. The coaching staff moved Joy Fawcett to the fullback line from midfield, and I moved into Joy's spot. Megan's unfortunate injury allowed me to start in 1991 in a position I had never played before. But Megan remained an important member of our team by channeling her energy into supporting us from the bench.

Of course, no team is totally harmonious. With anywhere from fourteen to twenty players on a team, a grab bag of personalities and ambitions, it is very difficult to blend into a cohesive unit. There are some people who are just so destructive that you don't want to play with them at all, but they are few and far between. Usually, between your coach and your teammates, you can work through any conflict and become stronger for it.

Because we do not have a professional women's league yet in the United States, the players on the National Team have been pretty much my only team since I left college. Many of us joined the team as sixteen- or seventeen-year-olds. We have basically grown up together. We went through high school and college as teammates, several of us got married, and some had kids. We won a World Cup together, lost a World Cup together, and regrouped to win an Olympic gold medal. While we've certainly had our ups and downs, you can't go through emotional milestones like that as a team and not form deep bonds. I couldn't have scored one goal without my teammates. I love them and always will.

But long before I became a national team player, I belonged to another team, one that helped me gain an appreciation for hard work and cooperation—my family.

I am one of six siblings, all equally talented in our own ways. Like all siblings do, we fought for the attention and praise of our parents. My oldest sister, Tiffany, found her calling in microbiology and went on to earn a Ph.D. and work in the Peace Corps. The weirdest stuff happens to my sister Lovdy; to hear her talk you'd think she was a stand-up comedian rather than a recruiting and marketing coordinator for a big law firm in Los Angeles. Caroline is Miss Congeniality. She can sing, cook, and write, but her real talent is making friends. I swear she could fill the soccer stadium at University of Texas at Austin, where she just finished college, with half the names in her address book. My brother Martin is the baby. He still thinks he can take me in one-on-one basketball. Hey, Martin, check the scoreboard. You should ask your real estate company for some time off to work on your hoops game if you ever plan to beat me!

I, of course, found my success on the soccer field. But we were all fortunate to have such incredibly giving parents who could nurture our individual talents while trotting the globe. You see, we moved around a lot when I was young, and being from such a big family, in which I always felt at ease, I struggled to fit in among strangers. For this shy kid, sports was an easy way to make friends and express myself.

When I say we moved around a lot, I mean to say I was a "military brat." My father was a colonel in the United States Air Force and was forever being assigned different posts. I was born in Selma, Alabama, but didn't stay there long enough to develop any affinity for the Crimson Tide. We moved four months later to Monterey, California. Before I was a year old, we packed our bags again and headed off to Florence, Italy. But just as I was getting my *ciao*s and *buon giorno*s down, we moved to Annandale, Virginia, when I was three and a half. When I was five, we were bound for Texas, where I would spend kindergarten through second grade in Wichita Falls. From third grade through fifth grade we lived in San Antonio, then it was back to Wichita Falls for grades six through ten. In the middle of my sophomore year, we relocated to Lake Braddock, Virginia, where I finished tenth grade and then graduated early, after my junior year, and went to Chapel Hill, North Carolina, to attend college. The day after I graduated from high school, my parents left for Rome! While my mom and dad became very good at packing boxes, I found stability on the soccer field.

Growing up, I did play on a couple of all-girl teams, but mostly I played with the boys. I enjoyed it and didn't think anything of being the only girl. It was either play with the boys or not play at all. Most important, playing with boys really helped me become competitive and develop that combative spirit I have today. I think it's my nature, but playing with boys reinforced my will to win and instilled a kind of fearlessness at an early age.

I truly believe that guys (much more so than girls) are taught to compete against one another and go after one another hard in practice and not apologize for success. As I got older, the boys started to get physically stronger and faster, and where I used to be one of the fastest on the team, at around fourteen or fifteen I had to start beating them tactically and technically, not just physically. That brought an entirely different dimension to my game, and having to make decisions at high speed helped me even more.

One of my main inspirations growing up was my older brother, Garrett, an incredible athlete himself. I was five and he was eight when he was adopted, and after he joined our family, I pretty much followed him wherever he went. Garrett always picked me for his teams in any sport, whether it was soccer, football, or volleyball at the beach. My mom would always say that I was his secret weapon. No one else would pick me because I was this quiet little girl. Boy, did they regret it. Later, they'd watch as I went out for a pass, sprinted past the defender, and caught the ball for a touchdown. Maybe I'd crack a line drive and scoot around the bases or shred defenses with a long dribbling run and score the winning goal. Needless to say, if they snickered when

Garrett picked his little sister, they weren't laughing at the end of the game.

As a role model for my athleticism and also as a competitor, Garrett embodied what I've always been reaching for. More than any other sibling, he shared my love of sports and competition and nurtured that important part of my life.

Garrett passed away in 1997 from complications arising from a bone-marrow transplant he underwent to combat a rare blood disease. It was an extremely difficult time for my family and me, but I was able to persevere through the pain and sorrow with the support of my teammates and the very lessons in courage and fortitude he helped me learn. Garrett was, and always will be, my inspiration.

Next to Garrett, coach Anson Dorrance has probably been the most influential person in my life. In my early years on the National Team and then all through college, he was the driving force behind my growth as a person and a player. On my college team he established an environment where I could get better every day. It was extremely competitive but in a positive way. He taught me that it was okay to want to be the best and pushed me toward that goal. He helped me understand that I had to be responsible for myself as well as for my teammates. In turn, they would watch out for me, both on and off the field. At UNC he forged a tremendous sense of family and community in a cauldron of hot competition. It was a unique situation, in which players went out and pounded on one another for several hours every day yet were as close as a family off the field.

When I arrived at North Carolina, Anson quickly became

At UNC, Anson Dorrance was both my coach and my legal guardian.

a father figure for me. As I was only seventeen and my parents were in Italy, he became my legal guardian. I grew very close to his family and soaked up every insight, every piece of advice I could. For four years of college, I pretty much picked his brain about soccer all day and learned how to build and maintain my confidence, which has always been a challenge for me.

During my junior year, I took most of the summer off before working at the UNC soccer camp. I was struggling. I was tripping over the ball and out of rhythm. Anson could see I was getting frustrated, so one afternoon he walked up to me and announced, "Mia, you're off balance." I stood there, confused, looking for some hidden meaning. "It's no riddle," he said, chuckling. "You're *literally* off balance."

So I started concentrating on keeping my center of gravity low and using my arms to steady myself when I made cuts or volleys. The next thing I knew I was back in rhythm, beating people and confident on the ball again. It was the simplest of things to correct. As players, when we are having a bad day, we tend to think in melodramatic terms, that we've lost it, that everything's gone wrong, but usually all you have to do is correct one small element of your game and everything else will fall into place. Anson understood that and, as always, knew how to get me back on track.

Anson saw me for the first time when I was fourteen and playing for the North Texas State Team at an Olympic Development tournament in Louisiana. I guess he liked what he saw because the next year, I found myself on my first trip with the National Team. Then on my second trip (to Taiwan, very exciting for a fifteen-year-old!) Anson pulled me aside after a game and uttered the craziest thing. "Mia," he said, "you can become the best soccer player in the world." I was flattered, but I didn't really believe him. Now, after I've won a bunch of championships in college, a World Cup, and an Olympic Gold Medal, people are saying I am. They're wrong. I have the potential, maybe, but I'm still not there. But because I can't believe what they say, because I'm not yet satisfied, someday I might prove them right.

TWO

Love the Game

To be a great soccer player, you must be in love with the game. You must love its culture, its nuances, the equipment, the skills it requires, the lessons it teaches you, and of course, the passion it creates among those who play and watch worldwide. In short, one of the most important parts of soccer is enjoying it. This makes for a kind of snowball effect: The more fun you have playing soccer, the more often you'll play; the more you play, the better you'll be; and the better you are, the more goals you'll score, the more games you'll win—the more you'll enjoy the game.

When you're young, the reasons you play are pretty

obvious. Soccer's a blast. You get to run around on a big green field with ten of your friends, kick a ball, wear cool uniforms (then cover them in mud), and, you hope, win a few games. Along the way, you acquire advanced skills, learn new tactics, and make plenty of soccer buddies, who, if you're lucky, will become friends for life. And whether you win or lose, you'll still get to go out for pizza after the game.

As you get to the higher levels of elite soccer, whether on a regional team or a national team, the recreational and social rewards of the game remain, but your love for fierce competition becomes an equally important reason to play. This intensity is what sets winners apart as you advance up

I admit it. Sometimes I go nuts when I score, but goals are so special they *must* be celebrated.

the ladder of soccer success. The goals you set for yourself, as an individual and as a team, become more ambitious, and achieving them is all the more gratifying. That's where the fun comes back into the equation.

This love of the game and competition is not something that can be taught. But it can flourish when your coach, your parents, and teammates create a competitive learning environment in practice, by making the game fun.

One key to appreciating the sport, which is often overlooked, especially here in the United States, is the value of studying elite soccer at the professional and international levels. Watching great players, in person or on TV, is without a doubt the best way to improve your game without actually playing. Not only do you get to see how beautiful a game soccer can be, but observing the great players in action gives you a visual picture to remember, one you can emulate next time you run out onto the field.

The soccer-playing girls of the United States have lacked role models for too long. You will see a ten-year-old girl on a basketball court dribble behind her back and then try to finger-roll the ball into the hoop. Where did she learn that? By watching Michael Jordan and his friends on TV every night and, more recently, the WNBA. Young European kids can watch professional soccer players on TV every day. Now it's time for American girls to have soccer role models of their own.

When the U.S. Women's National Team takes the field, we love looking into the stands at the sea of young girls in their team uniforms, chanting our names. It's a lot to live up to, serving as someone's example, but it's a great source of pride to us. I guess the main reason we feel that way is because when we were growing up we had very few female role models in sports. If you ask most of the veterans on the team, most of our sports idols were either outside of soccer or were men. Young players today are able to look up to our team, to outstanding collegiate teams like Florida, Santa Clara, and Notre Dame, not to mention my personal favorite, the Tarheels of North Carolina, and say, I want to be like Carla Overbeck, Kristine Lilly, Cindy Parlow, or Danielle Fotopoulos. I suppose a few want to be like me too. This is such an encouraging development for the future because, let's face it, there is only so much that a young girl can identify with in a male soccer player. You won't see many pasting on red goatees to look like Alexi Lalas.

When I was younger I wanted to be like Carin Gabarra. Carin is one of the best forwards to ever play the game. She was deadly at beating defenders off the dribble. I scored a goal during my junior year in the 1992 NCAA championship game against Duke on a play were I did two radical cuts with the ball before shooting. After the game, someone asked me where that move came from, and I said that if you play long enough with a talent like Carin Gabarra, you are bound to learn something.

But the only reason I got to study Gabarra's game was because I was fortunate enough to be on her team. Except for the odd World Cup game, soccer—men's or women's—wasn't televised back then. Now ABC, FOX, and ESPN regularly cover our games, Major League Soccer, and top international-league play. But far too few young female players seem to be watching. They're losing out.

If there is a game on, take some time to watch it, or if you have a VCR (and know how to program it), tape it. If you are

Carin "Crazy Legs" Gabarra, one of the best dribblers in the world, blowing past a Japanese defender in the quarterfinals of the 1995 Women's World Cup.

flipping through channels and stumble upon a game, watch it for a while. Get to know the players, their styles, and the teams. If you want to be a good player, it's not a bad investment of your time. And if your parents give you grief, tell them I said soccer is educational TV.

I vividly remember watching the 1986 World Cup on television. It was the first time that I had really followed the World Cup and focused on the games, the personalities, and the passion. I was hooked. Of course, Diego Maradona led Argentina to the championship, putting the team on his shoulders the way we all wish we could. His dribbling and passing in that tournament are forever imbedded in my mind.

Almost all the players on the National Team love to

watch soccer. Sometimes in the afternoon when everyone is resting after our morning session, a good European game will come on TV. Most of the time when we are in hotels, all the players are on the same floor. You know that everyone is watching because when a goal is scored, whooping and hollering erupt down the hallway. No telling what the other guests imagine is going on. Come to think of it, maybe that's why they always put us on the same floor. Later, at the team meal, there is the inevitable discussion of the highlights of the game, with Brandi Chastain and Julie Foudy trying to one-up each other in their obscure knowledge of the players. I guess we're just soccer junkies.

But best of all is attending games in person. When you are in the stadium, you see firsthand how fast the game is, how skillful the players are, and how they control the ball under intense pressure. You can also see how physically demanding the game is, with all the tackling and running. And the most exciting thing is witnessing the passion these players bring to the game and finding yourself swept up in the electricity of the crowd. Unless you're lucky enough to stand on the sidelines, you might not realize how fast, strong, and skillful these athletes are. When you watch basketball on TV, it looks as if they have so much time and space on the court. But when you sit courtside, time accelerates and space shrinks—the players look unbelievably tall; they fill the gaps with blazing speed and seem to leap into the rafters. Whether it's a club, college, or pro team, you simply must see quality soccer from field level to understand the difference.

Many kids say it's boring to sit and watch a ninety-minute soccer game, especially if they're not familiar with the players. I understand. Heck, I didn't avidly watch soccer until the '86 World Cup. To make it more interesting when you do go, study the game or at least part of the game. I don't mean take notes, as if you were in science class. Watch it like you would an MTV video before a school dance—you're trying to steal a few moves and get an edge. Pick out a particular player to focus on. Maybe choose one who plays your position. See what she does on and off the ball. See how she maintains possession, how she beats players, and how she makes an impact on the game. Watching Maradona's dazzling open-field runs in the '86 final and, later, Carin Gabarra with her whiplash cuts got me pumped. I couldn't wait to hit the field and try out a few of their moves.

On the National Team we watch a videotape of every game we play. Our coaches edit together positive and negative clips and ask us to analyze what went right and wrong. And video doesn't lie. In soccer, two scenarios are rarely the same. Often when your coaches try to describe something that happened in a game, it can be difficult to understand. They will say, "Well, if you had just made your run a little wider," and I'm thinking, "Well, I thought I did." And they say, "No, you needed to make it five yards wider." We go back and watch the videotape, and there it is in living color, and yes, if I had bent my run a little wider, I would have gotten in behind the defense.

Finally, let's go back to the beginning of the chapter and the most important part of soccer: fun. If you are not having fun, something is wrong, because soccer is all about enjoyment, no matter what level you play. If you are a casual player and you stop having fun because your interests go to other activities, it's not a big deal. But for those of us who live the game, sometimes the fun disappears, and that is a problem. Usually, it happens because you are obsessing on one aspect of your game. You become discouraged with every loss or put too much pressure on yourself to avoid making mistakes. You play tight.

You have to understand that in the course of a game negative things are going to happen. Soccer is extremely humbling in that respect. Anson Dorrance told us in college that whenever you play, you compete against two opponents. One is the team in the different-color jerseys, and the other is the game itself. Sometimes you can outplay your opponent,

Brandi Chastain leads the team in a Macarena warmup before a charity game supporting bone-marrow research.

but you can't beat the game. You outshoot a team 20–2, and yet they score one goal in the waning seconds and you lose 1–0. That's just the nature of soccer. But you can't dwell on the negatives. Yes, you always want to win, but if you only think about the result, you'll end up not enjoying the game.

What I'm saying is, don't exclude the process from the outcome; they do go together. If you understand how important one is to the other, you will enjoy yourself a lot more.

As much as we value winning, my teammates and I also cherish the process. We love the challenge of being the best, yet still striving to become better. We love the fact that the pressure is on us to win every game and that every team is gunning to knock us off the top of the world. We love wearing the colors of our country at home and on foreign soil. We love the kids who scream for us and young players who want to be like us. We love playing every day, and we love that we finally can make a living from the sport of soccer. In short, we love the game.

THREE

Love the Ball

The ability to make your skills come through under pressure in a game situation, to be able to control the ball with your feet as if they were your hands, is the essence of soccer. You must love the feel of the ball as you touch it with every surface of your cleats, your legs, your chest and head. Strive to make your skills so sharp and clean that they will not break down in the high-pressure atmosphere of the game. The only way to achieve this is to make the ball your constant companion, which means it should be at your feet mornings, afternoons, before and after practice, most days of the off-season, and, for the hard-core and superstitious, even when you sleep.

Go for the Goal

Over the years I've worked at hundreds of camps for young girls, and what has always distinguished the best players from the average ones is the great lengths they've gone to to become comfortable with the ball. I've heard of girls taking the ball to bed with them before a big game as if, by mere proximity to the ball, they could improve their touch! Hey, whatever works for you. Julie Foudy, for instance, found that by walking around with her Soccer Pal (a ball inside a mesh net attached to an adjustable cord you grip like a leash) she could practice juggling everywhere she went. Some of my teammates, much to the chagrin of their parents, would simply dribble the ball all over their house, nutmegging chair legs and sometimes their siblings. Look at their skills now!

I do love the ball, but sometimes you have to take a breather.

I can't emphasize enough how important it is for serious players to start young. If you have the base of your skills mastered by the time you are twelve, then your development will be determined by several factors, some you can control, some you can't. If you perform the skills correctly, then it is just a matter of how much soccer you play, how talented your teammates are, how tough the competition is, how much athletic ability you have, and how mentally and physically tough you are or will become.

But to really refine those skills, you must spend time with the ball. And the best way to do that is to simply play the game. As they say, the best coach in the world is the game itself. It teaches you what works and what doesn't. It tests your limits, challenges you to learn, and decides how good a player you are or can become.

When players go out and train on their own, they usually do it at half speed. This kind of training can be valuable, but it doesn't prepare you for competition, where you must perform at full throttle. So the trick is to schedule regular sessions of intense practice, while always leaving time to juggle and generally goof around with the ball.

One of the most important pieces of advice that I will give in this book is just to play soccer, against as good competition as possible. When you have all the basics down, it is in competition where you will naturally move on to more sophisticated runs, traps, dribbles, passes, and shots. The better the competition, the more the game will demand these advanced plays, and if your skills are sound, you will start to produce them. Playing against superior players forces you to learn and adapt. That environment will teach you new things every day and continually push you to improve. I first came on the National Team when I was only fifteen years old. There is no doubt that being thrown in with veterans almost twice my age greatly accelerated my development as a player.

One thing our National Team players have in common is that they all mastered the basic skills when they were very young and spent many hours working on their own. In addition to playing hundreds of full-sided games, they also played many small-sided or one-on-one games against friends. Soccer wasn't just their chosen sport, it was their hobby and their favorite recreation. I am not saying that if you don't have the basics mastered by age twelve, you will never be a good player, but I do believe bad habits are hard to break if you carry them into your teen years.

This is not a complicated idea. Developing your skills is simply a matter of picturing the correct form, then working hard to implement it through repetition. With the correct form, and if you play enough, whether you are short, tall, fast, or slow, you will most likely develop into a player who can contribute to the success of a team.

That's what makes soccer so unique—it's a democratic game that doesn't discriminate against those with lesser physical strength, build, or speed. After all, a girl of any size or shape can kick a ball. For instance, my mom was a ballerina, and following in her slippered footsteps was my first ambition. But I didn't have the grace or flexibility to be a ballerina (or a gymnast—yet another thwarted career path), so I quickly turned to other pursuits, including, of course, soccer. Thank goodness for that!

As you rise through the higher levels, the physical aspect of the game becomes more and more crucial. To be an impact player, your skills must be allied to speed and strength. However, if you're a step slow or a few inches shorter than the rest, you can often compensate for these liabilities by being extremely skillful with the ball.

When you talk to great players, all have stories about playing in their backyards, on the streets, or in pickup games during their youth. For as far back as I can remember, I played all the time at recess in grade school. It was mostly with the boys, but sometimes I could get the girls to play too. We played on the blacktop and concrete, so you really didn't want to fall down. But of course I came home with skinned knees on more than one occasion because I was going to do everything I could to beat the boys. We played using anything that happened to be available for goals—shoes, cans, or basketball poles. When the bell

Just one of the boys. Nice shorts!

rang, I didn't want to go back to the classroom. I'm sure in those early years that my mom thought soccer meant skinned knees and "often tardy" on my report cards.

In looking back, those school-yard games were probably a key in my development. I was able to dribble all I wanted. I had to learn to trap and pass on concrete, which helped me sharpen my skills, and as I mentioned earlier, always playing with boys made me push myself to a higher level. Those games on the hot Texas blacktop are one more example that the best way to develop skills is just to play.

By the time I joined the National Team, I realized I was way behind the veteran players technically, tactically, and mentally, and that I had to start putting in some extra work with the ball. So I'd go out to the park by myself every day and practice my skills for hours. Those lonely sessions helped me improve not only technically and tactically, but they also toughened me up mentally. I remember seeing the same couples over and over, walking through the park holding hands, just talking about their day. I'm sure they noticed me. Wouldn't it be cool if sometime they turned on the TV and did a double take: "Hey, Barb! Isn't that the young girl we used to see playing in the park all the time?"

FOUR

The Mental Game

A lot of kids ask me, "Mia, what is the most important thing for a soccer player to have? Is it a powerful shot? Is it the ability to pass accurately? Or should I be able to dribble the length of the field leaving defenders in my dust?"

In fact, it's none of those. Before you can perform the skills, before you even step on the soccer field to touch the ball, the most important attribute a soccer player must have is mental toughness. Before you can win, you must have the will to prepare to win.

The power of the mind is an incredible thing, one that can never be underestimated. The most amazing upsets you'll see in sports come from one team believing they can win despite the odds, willing their bodies to do mind-boggling things, and because of that, emerging victorious. It's likely the other team—the favored team—was not mentally prepared to play and it showed in their execution. This is a danger that all teams, both good and bad, face at every match. Which team will show up with the mentality it takes to win?

More often than anything else, mental toughness combined with physical toughness are the two parts of soccer that determine victory. Countless times in youth soccer, college soccer, and the pros, a team that was not nearly as talented as their opponent won the match because they contested every ball as if it were their last and scrapped until the very end.

For one of the most vivid examples of mental toughness in my career, I look back at the USA's third game of the opening round at the 1995 Women's World Cup in Sweden. In that game we had to come from behind four times, and three of those weren't even against the team we were playing! Talk about overcoming obstacles! It went something like this.

Heading into that third and final group match, we were tied with China on points, having each recorded a draw (against each other) and a win. We were also even on the first tiebreaker, which was goal difference, as both teams had scored two more goals than they had allowed, but China had the edge in the third tiebreaker, having scored two more goals than us. Put simply, to win the group, we had to beat Australia in our final group game by a larger score than that by which China beat Denmark in their final group game. If we both won by the same margin, which would mean our goal difference remained the same, China would win the group by virtue of more goals scored.

Both games were to kick off at exactly the same time.

We desperately wanted to win the group because that meant facing a second-place team from another group in our quarterfinal game. If we finished second in our group, we would have had the difficult task of playing the host team, Sweden, in front of a large, very blond crowd. Nevertheless, we were pretty confident going into our game,

Our historic victory over Australia during
the 1995 Women's World Cup was one of the greatest displays of
mental toughness I've ever seen from a soccer team.

because China had racked up four goals on Australia in a previous match. We felt sure we could put more than a couple of goals in the back of the net. But as I've said, you must prepare the same way mentally for every opponent, and looking back, perhaps we came into the game a bit soft, expecting the goals to come easy.

In the first half we didn't score at all. Our shots found the crossbar, their keeper made some spectacular plays, and we entered halftime deadlocked at 0–0. We quickly learned that China was tied with Denmark 1–1 at halftime, which meant that if that score stayed the same, we would only have to score one goal in the second half and then hold off Australia to win the group.

That's when things got hairy. Nine minutes into the second half, Australia scored, getting a great goal from their seventeen-year-old forward, Lisa Casagrande. Now we were down a goal and had just over thirty minutes to score twice!

What transpired in those remaining minutes was one of the greatest displays of mental toughness I have ever seen from a soccer team. Our coach, Tony DiCicco, had not started Julie Foudy or Carin Gabarra, but he brought them both at the beginning of the second half, and it paid off almost immediately when Julie scored a great header off my corner kick in the sixty-ninth minute. We now had about twenty minutes left to score one goal, and we would win the group—as long as China cooperated. Just three minutes later we got our second goal, as Joy Fawcett finished a rebound. We were up 2–1.

Our team liaison was getting updates from the China game on his cellular phone, and just as we were celebrating our second goal, the cell phone rang—China had scored to go up 2–1! We needed *another* goal to win the group. Tony yelled from the bench, "One more! We need another one!" We all knew what he meant, but now we had less than twenty minutes to score. We attacked and attacked, putting everything we had into getting another goal, but we couldn't find the net. Then, two minutes into stoppage time, I dribbled in the penalty box and was fouled. Penalty kick! Our captain, Carla Overbeck, stepped up and drilled the kick to go up 3–1.

The cell phone rang again, and although I was on the field, I was told that everyone on the bench screamed when they heard it. It was like a weird horror movie, *Attack of the Cellular Phone*! Needless to say, China had scored in the ninetieth minute, and Tony yelled again, "One more! Gotta have one more!"

Two minutes later, a full four minutes in stoppage time (let us now give thanks to the referee from Thailand for the generous allotment of stoppage time!), Debbie Keller scored our fourth goal. We had finally outlasted a team that wasn't even in the stadium!

It was a tremendous example of digging deep and finding the energy and power to accomplish something that seemed impossible. We scored four goals in the second half against Australia, every one crucial, and we did this because every player truly believed we could and took action to make it happen. That was mental toughness.

Mental toughness is also about how well you handle the ups and downs of your own game. You can have excellent skills and fitness, but when you blow an easy chance to score, flub a pass, or, if you're a 'keeper, let in a soft goal, your confidence can be severely undermined, wreaking havoc on your game. We've all been in situations when our confidence was shaky: down 3–0, feeling like you've lost your touch, and so spent all you want to do is lie down on the grass and wait for the final whistle. But if you believe in yourself, you can battle through these valleys.

You have to step on the field thinking, "I'm going to make an impact today," as opposed to thinking, "Mia, whatever you do, please don't give the ball away!" You have to be convinced that you are going to win every 50–50 ball, run yourself into the ground, still sprint some more, and finish your chances with authority.

But even if you play with confidence, how will you react when it seems as if fate, the referee, and your left foot are conspiring against you? Or you've dominated a team for eighty-seven minutes and a simple pass back to your keeper turns into an own goal and you lose 1–0? In short, how will you respond to adversity? Will you let it wreck your game, or will you keep your focus and push as hard as you can? Sometimes in big games you are matched up with a team that's more athletic or tactically superior, but unless they come prepared to stuff you in your own goal, if they relax even a little, they leave themselves vulnerable to your determined, relentless attack.

I can make very few guarantees in the game of soccer, but I can assure you that every time you lace up your cleats, there will be obstacles before you—some small, some large, some expected, and some out of the blue—that you must surmount to come out on top. The list of hurdles is endless, but it starts with the eleven players lined up on the opposite side of the field who want to knock you down and take the ball from you. Maybe the field is bumpy or narrow, the ball

I've got my game face on for our first match in the 1996 Olympics. I always walked out between Shannon MacMillian, number eight, and Michelle Akers, number ten.

doesn't have enough air in it, or the other team's parents are screaming at you. It could be raining, you could have stayed up all night studying for a test, you could be a little injured, or your best friend is on the other team. Your boyfriend is being mean to you, you have a ten-page paper due tomorrow, a dog ran on the field as you were about to shoot, or you just fell victim to a hard tackle and your shin and knee are stinging. Maybe you don't like your coach, your cleats are too tight, or you have a school dance to go to that night and you are going to be late. Maybe the last time you played against a defender she dominated you.

And that list doesn't even include your jitters before a

big game, or any game, and how you deal with those emotions. That is, pardon the expression, the kicker. You can't let any of these things affect your performance on the field. You must learn to focus, to find "the zone." That's what players with mental toughness do. Is it easy? Absolutely not. It is, in fact, one of the most difficult aspects of soccer and one I struggle with every game and every practice.

Many times, before games, fans call out my name for a picture or autograph, and sometimes I am not very responsive. And because of that I'm sure many think I'm conceited or stuck-up. Truth be told, not only am I a shy person, who will never be completely comfortable with all the attention, but also I know that to get focused, to find my zone, I have to tune out everything else. So next time you're at a game, here's my apology in advance. I promise to be more attentive afterward, especially if we win!

The ability to focus and stay mentally tough comes with time and experience. You must learn to differentiate between what is truly important and what can be dealt with at another time. Maturity gives you the ability to prioritize.

Learning how to deal with obstacles on the soccer field will no doubt help you off the field as well. Life, like soccer, isn't always fair. There are tackles from behind, your friends will sometimes let you down, referees miss calls, and sometimes your parents will blame you for things you didn't do. It is how you deal with these hurdles that to a large extent can determine how successful a person you are.

One of the most difficult situations I've ever had to deal with was the death of my brother Garrett. The painful emotional toll it took on my family and me was incredible. I missed the first two games of our Olympic Victory Tour in

April of 1997 to be with my family, but I knew that even though the game I love paled in importance compared to losing Garrett, I needed to get back on the field. The athletic field is where Garrett and I had so many great moments together, and I knew he would have wanted me out there. I knew also one of the best ways to deal with my grief was to play and to be with my teammates, so I joined the team in Milwaukee for our third game of the tour.

To focus mentally after that ordeal was one of the biggest challenges I've faced, and I must admit I really struggled to cope with my emotions and concentrate on soccer, but my teammates were remarkable in their caring for me and my family. There's no way I could have come back without their support and love, and I will always be grateful.

My brother Garrett was my inspiration and his son Dillon was his.

My first game back was against South Korea, and Milwaukee was deluged by rain. The field was covered in water, and you couldn't kick a ball further than five feet without it stopping dead in a huge puddle. Still, the fans came out. These were the same fans who had helped me organize a charity indoor soccer game the year before in Milwaukee to raise money for bone-marrow research. They packed the stadium despite conditions that might have canceled any other sporting event, and they cheered loudly when we took the field, or the lake, as it were.

The game started, and something amazing happened that I'll remember forever. Just thirty seconds into the match, the ball popped loose in front of the goal and I whacked it into the net. All the emotion from the fans and my teammates and from my ordeal rushed in at once. It was a truly overwhelming experience. I ran toward the stands and slid in the puddles before I was buried underneath a pile of soggy teammates.

It took a good dose of mental toughness combined with the support of my team to get me back on the field. It also showed me that you can overcome even the most tragic events if you put your mind to it and accept help from others. Mental toughness requires great patience and sacrifice. You must be willing to battle through the difficulties even if it's a long, arduous process like recovering from a serious knee injury. The way I have been taught to regain the mental edge when having doubts is to make life or the game as simple as possible. If you have all these insecurities or frustrations when you step on the field, you are giving yourself a hundred different reasons to fail. Those are pretty tough odds. Focus on what you know you can do. If you're having trouble finishing, concentrate on the pass. If attackers are getting the best of you, aim simply to contain them rather than take the ball away. Know what you're capable of on any given day, what you can count on; that's a philosophy I try to live by.

If you feel several elements of your game have slipped, zoom in on the most obvious. Say you're having trouble dribbling past opponents. Try holding the ball, shielding the defender, and looking for the pass. Each time you connect with a teammate, you'll be a little more confident controlling the ball. The next thing you know, you're not thinking of every part of the game, you're just reacting. Maybe you take a quick shot, beat someone with one move, or make a killer pass, and all of a sudden you're back on track. Do the simple things well, and then use that confidence to build up the rest of your game. As I've said, success breeds success.

A huge part of being mentally tough is leadership. It takes guts to lead by example, to assume responsibility for not only yourself but also your teammates. If you're having a bad game, it does no good to whine and complain. You have to focus on what you can do to help the team. Likewise, if your teammates are playing poorly, you have to lift them up. A team that has eleven leaders on the field, all taking it upon themselves to get the job done, is a team that's tough to beat. That's what we have on the U.S. Women's National Team.

Some lead by action, others by voice, and the best by both. I am more of a leader by action. Our captains, Carla Overbeck and Julie Foudy, are vocal leaders (we don't call her Loudy Foudy for nothing!) who shout out encouragement and instruction throughout the game. I'm not saying that everyone should be barking out orders, because then would be chaos. But everyone should be able to speak freely and honestly with their teammates. Yes, sometimes it gets heated and we yell at each other, but we don't take it personally. We know that we are doing it for the benefit of the team, and because of that, no one gets upset. If we do something wrong on the field, we expect nothing less than for a teammate to let us know about it. That's how you improve, by learning from your mistakes.

This "team before self" is an important part of mental toughness because it is often difficult to put other people's needs before your own. Selflessness is a key ingredient for a winning team. Everyone has to play her role, embrace it, and excel at it. Selfish people, those who are only concerned about how many goals they score, how many minutes they play, or who is playing with them, are liabilities.

One thing I've learned is that it helps to have your personal life organized so that when you step on the field, you are not being dragged down by other problems and are free to focus on the game. I know that to clear your personal slate of all conflict and worry is nigh impossible, but it's worth striving for nonetheless.

Mental toughness in soccer—reducing problems to their essence, confidence in adversity, and seeing the big picture—translates well to other difficulties you'll face apart from the game. A problem in life is like a defense in soccer: If you don't attack it, it won't go away. Break down problems aggressively like you try to break down defenses. It's the best way to solve them.

When it comes to mental toughness, the U.S Women's National Team is second to none. Every one of our players, from the starters to the reserves, is capable of unbroken concentration for the full ninety minutes. If one of the starters is substituted, there is no drop-off in intensity with the player replacing her. As I've said, one way to become mentally tough is through experience, which we have in abundance. Eight players have over one hundred caps, or games played, in a United States uniform. You will never see a national team, men or women, that has so many starters in the Century Club.

Most of the players have played matches in at least ten countries around the world (Kristine Lilly and I have played in eighteen!). We have played soccer in all kinds of conditions: on fields that looked suspiciously like cow pastures and in World Cup stadiums with turf as smooth as glass; on cold, rain-drenched mornings and balmy California afternoons; in friendly arenas where we were wildly cheered as well as in hostile environments where we were showered with insults and paper cups. My teammates and I have weathered sixteen-hour plane flights that arrive just before a match, been served some extremely unappetizing food, and stayed at fleabag hotels where you were afraid to walk out on the street without half the team around you.

On the field we've suffered brutal tackles from teams whose only recourse was to have us stretchered off the field, and we've endured games where the opponent pulled eight players back into their penalty area with no intention of truly competing but rather to frustrate our offense as much as possible. We have seen atrocious and biased refereeing and been forced to dress in locker rooms that would pass as condemned buildings in the USA.

Our ability to deal with all these obstacles and continue to win is undoubtedly one of our greatest strengths. We have a lot of players who embrace adversity and take pride

Hard challenges are part of the game. Take them in stride.

in persevering in inhospitable environments. There are no princesses on the National Team.

During my first year with the National Team, veteran players like April Heinrichs, Carin Gabarra, and Michelle Akers taught me about mental toughness through their play. We call it the "USA mentality." Nothing bothers us. Nothing gets in our way of being the best. We fight for one another every day in practice and in every game we play.

When we're not in camp pushing one another, I know that Julie Foudy is training in Southern California. I know that Michelle is killing herself in the Florida heat and that Shannon MacMillan and Tiffeny Milbrett are putting in the work they have to do in Portland. No one enjoys training alone, but we all do it. We do it because we know when we come together for a National Team game we don't ever want to let one another down.

When I was a youth player, I didn't have this attitude and work ethic. I would only practice with my team, but as you've heard before, I wish I knew then what I know now.

At UNC, Anson Dorrance, after spying me sprinting in that park all alone, left me a short, encouraging note: "The vision of a champion is someone who is bent over, drenched in sweat, at the point of exhaustion when nobody else is watching." His words had a profound effect on my attitude and lifted me up when my work ethic and resolve were lacking. They've also served as a definition of the kind of mental toughness we should all strive to possess.

First and foremost, you are accountable for yourself. No one is going to do the work for you. No one will roll you out of bed at 5:00 A.M. to run. You alone have to make that decision. It's a challenge to get out there on the field, run the sprints, and train with the ball when there is no one else around. But that's when it's going to make the biggest difference and have the most impact, because while everyone goes to practice, not everyone is putting in the extra hours. Remember, this is what sets champions apart. They do what it takes to be the best no matter how painful, how boring, or how difficult it is to find the time.

This is the USA mentality that we try to instill in all the

young players who join the National Team. We also like to call it "warrior mentality." To the National Team, it means that once we step on the field, we are coming after you with a take-no-prisoners attitude. We are not going to sit back and take all your best shots and then react. We will attack and impose our game and our style on you, make you react to us.

There are two games in our history that best illustrate what was and what was not the warrior mentality. In the 1995 Women's World Cup in Sweden, instead of creating our own chances, we sat back and let Norway dictate the game, hoping that they would make mistakes and leave the door open. We played afraid, we lost the game 1–0, and Norway took away our title as World Cup champions. On that day they were clearly the better team. They were mentally tough and we weren't.

In 1996 at the Olympics we vowed not to let that happen again, and we flat-out went after Norway in the semifinals. As I'll detail later, after the '95 game, they'd rubbed our faces in it. This was a grudge match, and we came in determined to get some payback. We wanted to force them to play our game, and in front of more than 65,000 people, we did. We were down 1–0 in that game, tied the match in the second half, and then in sudden death overtime, when our mental toughness was strained from exhaustion, we reached a little deeper and pulled out the winning goal.

It doesn't matter whether we are ahead or behind in a game. It doesn't matter what country we are in, what surface we are playing on, or what opponent is across the field. Nothing stands between us and success but our own will to win.

FIVE

The Physical Game

Anyone who says soccer is not a physical game has never played or watched up close. If they had, they would have seen great athletes running at top speed, kicking the ball and one another, sometimes on purpose, sometimes not. They would have seen players clash in the air for head balls. They would have seen all the grabbing, pushing, and tripping that goes on as teams battle to score and stop each other from scoring. Soccer is perhaps the most physical women's game in today's sporting world. Heads butt, bodies go flying, and cleats shred ankles, shins, and knees all over the field as twenty-two players fight for that precious ball. The extent to which you will sacrifice your body in a game is often the difference between who wins and who loses.

Fitness, speed, and strength: The complete player must possess all three. Many players possess only one or two of these assets. There are players who are fast and can run for the full ninety minutes but are not strong enough to fend off opponents. There are players who are very strong and in good shape but just not fast enough to get behind a defender. When you have all three of these assets and add mental toughness, you are someone who can really make an impact on the game.

Fitness is one part of your game that you have complete control over. Dedication to being in top shape can significantly improve all parts of your game and, perhaps most important, help avoid injury. If you are in the kind of shape that we all strive for, a state of physical fitness where your first sprint is as fast and hard as your last, then near the end of a game, when the opponent is wilting, your speed will be even more productive. So many games are decided in the last fifteen minutes because mental and physical fatigue lead to mistakes.

Speed is one of the most important weapons a player can have in the women's game. Countless youth and college teams are successful because they have fast players. Speed is tremendously difficult to defend, as it can only be countered by disciplined positioning and defenders of like quickness. Since I was a little girl, I have always been one of the faster players. My ability to explode into my dribbles and pull away from defenders has helped me score many of my goals.

Strength in soccer is the ability to hold the ball with a defender on your back, to push through tackles, and to maintain your balance when running with the ball even as a defender is putting her shoulder into you. Strong players can jump higher, muscle opponents away to win head balls, and dish out physical punishment as well as absorb it. This means that at any time during a game you are not afraid to lay down a hard tackle, so your opponent knows you are there and will be again the next time she goes for a 50-50 ball. I would never advocate playing dirty or fouling on purpose, but being able to hit hard and clean on your tackles is definitely one of the keys to playing good defense and controlling the game.

Since the 1995 World Cup, when we lost to a stronger, tougher Norwegian team, we have been dedicated to building physical strength through weights and running. We now have some of the biggest, most fearsome players in the world in 5-foot-11 forwards Danielle Fotopoulos and Cindy Parlow, who are both lethal combinations of size, speed, and power. Marking either of those players for a whole game no doubt means ninety minutes of pain for any defender. Our goalkeeper, Briana Scurry, has made tremendous strides in her game from weight training and is now ruling the air in the penalty box. I would say that almost every core National Team player has gained valuable muscle in the last several years. This is important to our success, because despite Danielle and Cindy, we average about 5 feet 6 inches and are subject to a great amount of physical pounding every game.

Michelle Akers, however, might be the toughest woman alive. Some of her collisions on the soccer field make me cringe. I often think the hits she takes would wreck a mortal woman, or at least my 5-foot-5 frame. But Michelle doles out punishment just like she receives it, and no one is more aggressive at winning tackles on the ground or head balls in the air. Her play in the Olympic semifinal showed just what she is made of—half iron muscle, half iron will. Michelle was playing her fourth game in eight days, which with her Chronic Fatigue Syndrome is an incredibly difficult task. Many people with that disease have a hard time with nine-to-five desk jobs, but here is Michelle playing world-class soccer!

As tough a competitor as Michelle is on the field, she's equally nice off it.

Because Norway hit so many long balls, her heading was vital to our winning the match. She won head ball after head ball, scrapped for every loose ball in the midfield, and won some crunching tackles. I could see in her eyes that she was starting to lose her strength but also that she was trying to push through it. Her body kept saying stop, but her will was stronger. I have never seen such physical sacrifice from a player. Michelle was running on fumes, so much so that at halftime she had to take intravenous fluids in the locker room. It was a bit scary.

But I'll take Michelle on her last gasp over almost any player in the world, and when it counted most in that game, she came through like a true champion. Time was running out. We were down one goal with fourteen minutes left when a Norwegian player was called for a hand ball in the box. Penalty kick! No one made a move toward the ball. There was no doubt who would step up to take the kick—it was Michelle's to put away.

On the biggest kick of her life, in front of a packed stadium with all our hopes and dreams on the line, Michelle slammed the ball into the left corner with unbelievable pace and authority. She mustered every bit of strength and focus she could to make that kick and probably used up whatever she had left celebrating, jumping up and down as we ran to embrace her. With Michelle's goal, we regained some momentum and went on to win the game in sudden death overtime. Shannon MacMillan scored the winning goal, but I think we all felt that the lion's share of the credit for the victory belonged to Michelle, whose hustle and grit had made the difference.

Those who watch the U.S. Women's National Team have surely seen that our forwards (and that includes me) are often victims of rough play. There are a few countries who really come after me, and going into a match with them, I know I'm in for a physical afternoon. Because our attackers are talented dribblers, and because we have numerous players blessed with speed and strength, defenders are often caught off balance and will stick out a leg to chop us down. At the highest levels of soccer, the space gets tighter and the defenders get nastier as you move closer to the goal. We are probably one of the most fouled teams in the world, and while at times it does get frustrating, we try to remember it's just part of the game. You must be able to withstand the punishment, get up off the ground after each tackle, and have no fear of running again at that same defender who just sent you barreling to the turf. Eventually you'll wear them down.

The fact is, all international matches are physical. When two countries meet on the athletic field, national pride is on the line and participants tend to raise their level of play. The most physical women's international match I ever played in 1995 on our Road to Sweden tour to prepare for the 1995 Women's World Cup. We opposed a fired-up Brazil team in Tacoma, Washington. It was the first time we'd faced Brazil in four years, and the previous match had been at the 1991 Women's World Cup in China, where we cruised to a relatively easy 5–0 victory. Brazil is a country that takes tremendous pride in its soccer, and I think they were really looking to prove they were a much different team from the one we'd faced in '91. They were, and I had bruises to prove it.

The game was in a high school football stadium, and the field was one of the narrowest we've ever played on. There just wasn't enough space to work free of the defenders; they were always on top of you. Combine the lack of maneuvering room with Brazil's aggressive defensive strategy (more or less based on hacking Michelle Akers and me every time we touched the ball), and we had a war on our hands. I don't think it helped that I scored on a breakaway about two minutes into the game, because it just got them even more ornery than they were at the start.

The referee did a poor job of keeping the game under control, and we started to retaliate, which of course is the wrong thing to do, but in the heat of the game sometimes you lose your cool. I remember Michelle laying out a

Kristine Lilly (a.k.a. The Queen of Caps) has played more times for her country than any man or woman in the history of soccer.

Brazilian player, and when Michelle tackles you, you know it. As the player rolled around on the ground and complained to the referee, Michelle swirled her finger as if to say, "What comes around goes around."

As the game wore on and the fouls mounted, players on both benches were on their feet, angrily yelling at the referee and the opposing team. During the second half I trapped a ball right in front of our bench. As I slowed to collect the ball, my back was to the field, and I could feel the Brazilian player coming from behind me. I knew I was about to get whacked, so I tried to jump clear. But I was a second too late, and she caught me hard in the back of the legs with both cleats, driving me into our bench.

Everyone went nuts, especially our coach, Tony DiCicco, who gets particularly upset when foul play becomes dangerous. I swear it was as close to a bench-clearing brawl as I have ever seen in women's soccer. Both teams left their benches and formed a yelling, pushing scrum at midfield. Luckily, cooler heads prevailed and Tony avoided an international incident by opting not to punch the rather hot-headed Brazilian coach.

While the U.S. team will never back down from physical play on the field, we know the best way to get back at a team is to score goals. Retaliating will do you no good—let the other team get the red cards. A victory is the best way to show who is the better team and that rough play is not a winning tactic. Tisha Venturini scored in the second half, and I scored a bookend goal in the final minutes of the game to match my opener. We won 3–0. And oh, how sweet it was.

While that match in Tacoma was brutal, I must say I still have great respect for the Brazilian team. We've played them several times since, and they are always tough, but it's great to know we've been able to meet their physical toughness with some physical and mental toughness of our own and persevere for the victory.

You can't let the fouls upset you and throw you off your game. If you are not running your hardest with full confidence when that chance to score materializes, you will be less likely to put it away. It's a battle of wills. Whose body or mind will last the longest?

Life is about competition, and the sooner you learn that, the better equipped you'll be to survive and succeed in the world. Soccer teaches you these lessons. You certainly cannot win every game, and learning how to deal with losing, and how to bounce back, is just as important as competing hard to be a winner.

In college at North Carolina I learned valuable lessons in mental and physical toughness from Anson Dorrance. Every practice, we were graded and ranked on our performance in drills. The results were posted in The Hut, our soccer building, and it became a matter of pride: I, for one, did not want to see my name on the bottom of any list! This created an environment of intense competition, forcing us to be mentally focused and physically tough for an entire practice. And of course, that carried over into games.

Often the true measure of a player's impact on the game is her work rate and ability to win the ball. The work rate, the willingness to run the entire game, is a measure of her stamina and mental toughness. The ability to win tackles and balls in the air and to chase down opponents is a measure of her physical toughness.

Some players are naturally stronger and faster than others. The good news is that everyone can improve through intensive training, whether alone or with the team. By working out on a consistent basis—lifting weights, running, and playing lots of soccer—you can bridge the gap. While young players shouldn't lift serious weights until their late teen years, weight lifting does have great benefits. Speed coaches can help you improve your running technique and make your first step more explosive. On the National Team we have a great strength-and-fitness coach named Dave Oliver. Not only does he work us until we're ready to drop, but he also helps develop our off-season regimen, which, frankly, can sometimes seem sadistic. Last chapter I told you how mentally tough it is to train alone, but, believe me, it's also physically tough! (See my log, opposite.)

The American women have long had an edge in the physical part of the game, but we are well aware that the rest of the world is getting more athletic and catching up to us. In the past we could win games based solely on our fitness, speed, and strength, but those days are gone. If two teams meet that are basically even in the physical aspects of the game, then it will come down to talent and mental discipline.

I would hope that young girls now know that it is okay to be tough, to be competitive, and to defeat an opponent. Girls should be encouraged to fulfill their athletic potential and to be winners. One of the most gratifying aspects of being part of the U.S. Women's National Team is that we are constantly showing that women can be hypercompetitive and supertough while still being positive role models.

A PAGE FROM MY TRAINING LOG

<u>Nov. 14</u>
- Sprint Series (40's, Cones, 120)
    - Times: Set 1: 46, 47; 34, 34, 17, 18
    - Set 2: 47, 48, 34, 34, 18, 18
- Coervers
    - Inside-out, ~~Inside~~ out-in, etc..

Approx. 18 yd.
Approx. 15 yd.
GOAL   small goal

① Back pedal to line, sprint to cone,
   Figure 8 w/ball → shoot to small goal
          (4x each foot)
② Back pedal to line, 5 tuck ups,
   figure 8 w/ball → shoot. (4x ea. foot)

③ Jump over cone 5x, back pedal
   to line, sprint to ball,
   power shot to small goal.
          (4x each foot)

- Weights
    - back, tris, leg extension, calves (3x10)
    - situps (5x30)

<u>Nov. 15</u>
- lvl w/ Christiaan
    10 x 15 yd. field; 1.5 yd. goals
    15 min.
- Shooting
    - across body, pressure shooting, 1-touch finishing

<u>Nov. 16</u>
- Coerver Series
- Form Running
    - striders, butt-kicks, high knees, bounding (2x 25 yd.)
    - jumps: side/side, front/back, 1 leg, height (30x)
    - W-sprints (2 sets of 5)
    - reaction sprints (10 yd. 10x)

PART II

On the Field

SIX

Trapping

The Ball Is Your Servant

You can call it trapping, collecting, receiving, or controlling, but by whatever name, it is still the most important skill in soccer. During a game the ball comes at you in a hundred different ways at a hundred different speeds and a thousand different angles. Oh yeah, and it's spinning too. You have to be able not only to control the ball, but at the same time prepare it in the best position to make your next move, whether it be a pass, a dribble, or a shot.

If you have difficulty trapping a ball, you will always have trouble executing the other skills you need to excel in soccer. Make a less-than-perfect trap, and you will spend time and energy trying to get that bouncing ball down to the grass. Or you might have to chase the rolling ball all over the field, while defenders are running at you full tilt with no other intention than to separate you from the ball. And sometimes that can hurt. What hurts more, though, is that without the ball, you can't pass or dribble. And if you can't pass or dribble, you can't get in position to shoot and score. And if you can't score, you can't win. So in a game, at that moment when the other twenty-one players and every fan is looking at you and the ball comes to you, you want to keep it. It's a precious thing. The less time you spend controlling the ball, the more time you have to choose the best option on the field.

You must be able to trap with all surfaces. Here, I bring the ball under control with the outside of my left foot.

For all skills in soccer, repetition is vitally important. The more you do something, the more proficient you become. There is no better example of this than trapping. At first it may be very difficult to bring a speeding soccer ball under control with your feet, your thighs, your chest, even your head—with everything except what comes naturally, your hands. But as you practice and play, it will get easier. And if you work hard enough, soon that ball will be your servant, willing to do anything you ask.

This may sound funny, because trapping doesn't seem nearly as glamorous as shooting or dribbling, but sometimes I find it to be one of the more satisfying soccer skills. Maybe that's because it's one of the most difficult. To be able to trap a 40-yard pass out of the air with the instep of your foot and have it stop on a dime—well, I'll never stop enjoying it.

On the U.S. Women's National Team my teammates and I often strike long balls as part of our warm-up routine before practices and games. To see a group of women trapping long passes out of the air with grace and style kind of reminds me of a choreographed dance troupe. Every move is clean, powerful, and purposeful. It's as if they have been doing it all their lives, which I guess they have!

There is a moment that sticks in my mind as the first time I realized the importance of trapping. I was five or six, and a goalie (we called them goalies back then) was taking a goal kick while I was standing just outside the penalty box. When you're that young you can't kick very far, and the penalty box is only about 10 yards long. The goalie kicked the ball, and it headed right at me. I probably would have been able to trap it because it wasn't struck *that* hard, but all I could do was think, "Oh my gosh! Here comes the ball!" Instead of using a surface, like my thigh, chest, or foot, I just jumped in front of the ball, and it hit me smack in the stomach, knocking the wind right out of me. I was momentarily stunned, but I still swung at the ball. Groaning and gasping for breath, I couldn't believe it when the ball rolled into the net. My first garbage goal!

It was more a stomach ball than a trap. I was lucky to get my foot on the ball, much less score. It certainly helped that the kid taking the kick was the goalie and was way out of position.

If I met that kid today, I doubt he'd be saying that Mia Hamm scored on him when he was six. More likely he'd say that when Mia Hamm was six, she couldn't trap the ball. Well, I remember thinking that if I didn't want to keep getting nailed in the stomach, I'd better learn how to trap correctly. I mean, how often was the goalkeeper going to kick the ball right at me? And if he did, I certainly didn't want to get creamed again.

Ever since I started playing, trapping has been something I've had to work on, and to this day I still need improvement. At any position but especially at forward—the position I've played most of my life—the ability to hold the ball is vital to the success of your team. When the ball is passed to you, you must be able to keep control of it, so that your teammates can advance up the field and your team can get more players into the opponent's attacking third. The point is, whether you're intercepting a pass from an opponent, collecting one from your teammate, or just in the right place when the ball squirts out from a swarm of players, you rarely receive a perfect ball. The pass might not have the best pace, it might not be that accurate, or it might be bouncing a bit too much. Plus, you are almost always under pressure from a defender. Being able to bring the ball under control in order to make your next touch an efficient one can mean the difference between having the time to shoot and having your shot stuffed by a defender.

If you watched the 1998 World Cup from France, you

were lucky enough to see what might be the ultimate trap, if there is such a thing. In the last minute of the quarterfinal match between Argentina and Holland, with the score 1–1, Frank de Boer hit a long pass to Holland's star forward, Dennis Bergkamp. Dennis is everything you want in a forward. Strong and fast, he can hold the ball on the forward line and is a great finisher. On this play, Dennis was racing flat out with a defender at his side when the ball reached him. Effortlessly, he brought the ball down in the penalty box with the laces of his right foot and cut it back inside with his next touch, losing his defender in the process. Then, from a sharp

Sometimes you have to just wrap it and play.

angle, he struck a shot with the outside of his right foot, bending it into the far corner past Argentina's goalkeeper, Carlos Roa. Roa was no doubt stunned by the grace and simplicity with which Dennis could make such a difficult play.

Dennis Bergkamp, eat your heart out!

And to win the game and send his team to the semifinals, no less! The Dutch team swarmed him in a huge dogpile of orange jerseys. What a great soccer moment!

In college I had a similar moment of inspiration. The ball came over my inside shoulder, kind of like the pass to Dennis, and I brought it down out of the air smoothly as I cut at top speed toward the goal. With my next touch I took a shot, but unlike Dennis's, it went wide. No dogpile for me. Still, I remember being really surprised that I had even brought the ball under control in that situation. It wasn't something I'd planned, it just happened because of all the years of trapping practice and repetition in training and games. I remember thinking, "That was pretty good!" And I don't think that very often.

Acquiring skills is a process of evolution. When you get really good at the basics, they will become second nature, and one day the game will present you with a difficult ball that you bring under control without thought or trouble—a truly great feeling.

So I went from taking a ball in the gut and scoring to making a brilliant trap and missing the goal. Sometimes that's just how the game of soccer works. Still, the point was made with me. I'll take a great trap over a ball drilled in the 'ol breadbasket anytime, because as you move up the ranks in soccer, you are less likely to get gifts in front of the goal. You will need to be able to control that ball to be effective, to have more fun, and to help your team win.

Technique

When I work with youth players, the most effective example I use in teaching trapping is the idea of an egg or water-balloon toss. If you stick your hands out or move fast toward the balloon or the egg, you will probably end up all wet or covered with yolk. You must think about cushioning the egg or the balloon with your hands. It's the same with trapping. If you stick your foot or thigh out there stiffly, the ball is probably going to bounce off in who knows what direction. But if you *cushion* the ball—if you absorb a little of its pace—it will settle into your body and be prepared for your next touch. This is true with whatever surface you are trapping with, and there are many. You must learn how to do this with the inside and outside of both feet, with the top and bottom of both feet, with your thighs, your chest, and even your head.

Balance is also vital in making a good trap, and some people have better equilibrium than others. You must have your feet under you in order to make a quality trap and be

| Inside of foot | Outside of foot |

prepared for your next move. If you are stumbling, falling, or on your heels, it will be tough to trap well on a consistent basis. That's why it's smart to be moving to the spot where it will be easiest to trap the ball, whether it comes in the air or on the ground. And you must always move to the ball. Wait until it gets to you, and you will almost certainly be too late. This is something that can't be coached. You must play the game to hone these instincts.

Perhaps the most important thing to remember when trapping with your feet is that you have to lock your ankle. Whenever your foot makes contact with the ball, whether it's trapping, passing, dribbling, or shooting, you must lock your ankle so that you have maximum control of the ball. You must play the ball or the ball will play you!

If you are trapping with the inside of your foot, make

sure that your toe is pointed up and your ankle is locked.

If you're trapping with the outside of your foot, make sure that your toe is pointed slightly down and, of course, that your ankle is locked.

When trapping with the instep or your laces, make sure that your toe is pointed down to give the ball a nice surface to settle on, and don't forget to lock that ankle!

I want to drive this point home because so often when I work with kids, I see way too many toes flopping around. You will never succeed trapping unless you train your body to lock the ankle. The cushioning part doesn't come entirely from your foot. It comes from your legs and your hips giving just a bit to take the steam out of a hard pass, or putting a little force into a slow moving ball to push it where you want it to be.

The spin turn is a move that should be mastered early.

To be effective, you must move the ball in the most positive direction for your team (i.e. away from pressure and into open space). This can include trapping the ball on the run as you are moving forward or backward or changing direction. Often you are turning as you trap—turning to find an open teammate or turning to goal—and you must learn to trap and guide the ball at the same time.

Turning the ball as you trap must be done with the inside and outside of both feet. The key is to keep your feet moving so that as the ball comes to you, you're already partially turned and you can push, slice, or spin the ball in that direction. Being able to master traps like this is crucial to opening up the maximum number of options for your next move. As you get better, you can make traps on the move while letting the ball run through your legs and guiding it with the inside of your heel, or cutting it sharply as you turn to beat an onrushing defender. As always, watching those who have mastered their skills and then practicing on your own or with your team is the best way to improve.

Thigh trapping can be difficult because the "sweet spot" on your thigh is not that big. In addition to the cushioning motion of drawing your thigh back and almost gently laying the ball

Thigh trap

Sight the ball,

trap it on your chest…

…and collect it as it falls to the ground.

on the ground, you must remember to trap the ball toward the top of your thigh on the area that has the most muscle. The lower part of your thigh, near the knee, is a bit harder, and trapping there is more likely to make the ball bounce away.

One very important thing to remember when trapping with your thigh or your chest is that you will have to trap the ball twice: the first time to take the ball out of the air, and again when it drops to the ground. You want your first trap to take most of the speed out of the ball so it will fall to your feet without too much bounce. But there will always be a little, so you must be balanced and ready to smooth that ball out on the turf after a thigh or chest trap. Often the sole of your foot works well for this trap, but you must be prepared to use any part of your foot.

Chest trapping is done as much with the legs as with the chest. As with any ball in the air, you must first move quickly to where the ball is going to land. This is important so that you don't have to reach to make a trap. Reaching will almost always leave you off balance and make bringing the ball to the ground much more difficult. Once you are in good position to trap, remember that it's your legs that give you the ability to cushion the ball. As the ball comes to you, bend your knees and lean your body backward slightly so that your chest becomes a kind of plateau. Your arms must be up, with your elbows aiming out, not only for balance but also to create a pocket on your chest to catch the ball.

Brandi Chastain is one of the best trappers on the National Team. As a forward on the 1991 Women's World Cup Team, she was a member of the first world champion team in women's soccer, but didn't get called up to play for the National Team for about four years after that. During those four years she had the character to keep playing and working toward getting back to the highest level. Because of her great skills and versatility, when she returned to the National Team in 1996, this time as a defender, she was able to make a tremendous impact on the team and played a huge role in our winning the Gold Medal at the 1996 Olympics in Atlanta.

Brandi's a bit of a daredevil, but she always comes out with the ball.

Brandi takes a lot of pride in her trapping ability. She reminds me of those guys I grew up with on my youth soccer team who were always trying to outdo each other with ball tricks and fancy stuff. Brandi is like that all the time. She's able to take the ball down with all parts of her body from her chest to the back of her heel and then play a great pass with the next touch. One of the reasons she's so good is that she works on it constantly, harder than anyone else, even in the intensely competitive atmosphere of the National Team training camp. Having the ball totally under control gives Brandi incredible confidence—confidence bordering on cockiness, to be sure. Often, in the penalty box, she'll trap the ball on her chest and dribble it out of trouble in spots where most players might boot it out and risk losing possession. I'm not recommending this course of action all the time, as a good 40-yard clearance is often called for, but the value of keeping possession can never be underestimated. Brandi's unique style probably drives our coach, Tony DiCicco, nuts sometimes, and I know it makes goalkeeper Briana Scurry crazy, but the thing about Brandi is, she always comes out with the ball.

Great skills will give you confidence on the ball, and confidence breeds creativity. Once you feel free to be inventive on the field, you will try new things and constantly test yourself, and that is when you really improve.

BRANDI SAYS: I believe that every player on the field should not only be proficient in trapping the ball but should *want* the ball even under the greatest pressure. If you're worried about making a mistake or you aren't confident with your touch, you will almost always lose the ball. The game of soccer is all about rhythm, deception, trickery, and *fun*. To truly enjoy all the game has to offer, the last thing you should be worrying about is whether or not you can bring a ball under control. Instead, you should be dissecting the opposing defense in your mind, so when the ball does come you're relaxed and ready to execute your next move. *Don't* fight the ball!

Every good player starts with the basics, and I usually work on trapping twice a week. For example, I will focus on preparing my first touch into a space, away from any defenders but close enough so that I can make a pass or take a shot with the second touch. I also

Trapping Games/Drills

Keys to remember:
- Emphasize "cushioning." Think of catching an egg or water balloon.
- Trap into your body; keep the ball close.
- Work on all surfaces and both feet.
- Get the ball under control as quickly as possible.
- While training, always progress toward trapping a moving ball while moving yourself.
- Never forget to lock that ankle!

---

work on shielding, which is a good exercise for forwards who often find their backs to the goal and for backs, like me, who often are facing their own goal on defense. Of course, when you trap the ball all depends on what part of the field you're in, where the closest defender is in relation to you, and whether you're winning or losing the game.

The second training session focuses on receiving the ball in different situations, using all surfaces. If you don't have a partner to work with, use a wall. Always be on your toes! Never be surprised when the ball comes your way.

Last, it's important to remember that having fun is the B.L., or bottom line. Soccer is a great teacher of life's little lessons, but it's not life. Always leave the field knowing that you've given your best and that you've learned something.

The Wall

It sounds too simple, but finding a wall with some open space in front of it (not your living room!), kicking the ball off the wall and then trapping it is one of the best ways to work on this skill. The harder you kick the ball, the faster it will come off the wall and the less time you will have to react. You can test yourself by kicking it at all speeds and different angles with different bounces. While kicking off the side of the house or garage may be annoying to your parents, a short session of "kick-back" every day can really improve your skills. This is also something you can do by yourself when you can't find someone to play with. I spent many hours on the racquetball court at the University of North Carolina just hammering balls off all the walls and trapping them, and it no doubt helped my skills immensely. As you get better, you can work on your passing and shooting against the wall as well.

The Pelé Series

During every training camp for the U.S. Women's National Team, at some point we run through the Pelé Series. If we don't do it with the team during warm-up before biting into the meat of a training session, then we'll do it at the end when Tony gives us ten minutes to do whatever we want on our own. That we do this drill is a testament to the fact that even elite players still need to work on the basics sometimes. It's simple but very valuable.

You'll need a partner and a ball. Face each other about 3 to 4 yards apart. It's best to start doing the drills while standing basically in one place, but as you get better, you can move forward and backward.

Each series starts with your partner playing the ball to you. Do ten repetitions, then switch places with your partner. Always start with your strong foot (designated here as the right), but don't neglect the other foot. It will benefit you greatly down the road to play with both feet. Almost every National Team player is able to perform all the skills at a high level with both the right and left foot.

1. Have your partner pass a ball on the ground. Trap with the outside of your right foot, and play it back to her with the inside of your right foot. Now trap with the inside of your right foot, and play it back to her with the outside of your right foot. Switch to your left foot, and work on various traps and passes with the inside and outside of both feet.

2. As you progress in the drill, from about 5 yards away, have your partner throw balls to you with her hands. Trap the ball with the inside of your strong foot, smooth out the ball on the ground if you need to, and play it back to her on the ground. Try using your other foot and different surfaces.

3. Have your partner throw the ball with a little loft on it, trap on your thigh, clean it up, and pass it back on the ground. Switch thighs and feet, but make sure you are making a deliberate effort to trap with a particular thigh and pass back with a certain foot.

4. Have your partner toss the ball high in the air, then trap it on your thigh and knock it back into her hands

out of the air without its bouncing. Do this with your chest and head as well.

5. Have your partner toss you the ball, then kick it back to her hands with a single touch.

That's the Pelé Series. Once you have the skills and confidence to hit your partner's hands every time, while moving or standing, you are well on your way to mastering trapping. Simple as it seems, the Pelé Series is hard work, and it takes many hours of practice to avoid having to chase the ball all over the field. As with everything, don't get frustrated. Keep working hard and you'll get it.

The Circle Series

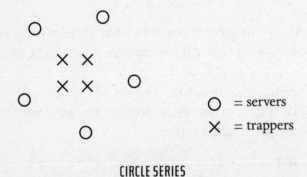

CIRCLE SERIES

Using the Circle Series, you can work on trapping with the whole team. One half of the team forms a circle and trains the other half, who are inside the circle. Everyone on the outside of the circle has a ball. The outside players toss the ball to the inside players, who are constantly moving and sprinting toward a player with a ball. The players on the inside can trap the ball with whatever surface the coach calls out, then play the ball back to the server and immediately go in search of anther ball. After several minutes, the servers become the trappers. The grid size can be 15 × 15 yards or larger, but it must have enough room for the players to move and receive the ball without it bouncing off too many teammates. The constant crisscrossing and darting of the players simulates a game and helps you improve your trapping under the pressure of movement.

2 Training 1

2 TRAINING 1

Begin in a line with the two players on the outside facing the player on the inside. The players on the outside alternate tossing or passing the ball with their feet to the player in the middle. The player in the middle receives from one, traps it, then kicks the ball back to the player who served her. As soon as the middle player returns the ball, the moment it leaves her foot, the other outside player should serve her another ball. This forces the middle player to be in constant action—trap, pass, turn, trap, pass, turn. Start with your feet, and progress to the thighs, chest, and head. You can break the drill down into sets, focusing on each surface before switching an outside player to the middle. Beware! This can be very fatiguing, and it's best to switch positions after each set, but of course working on your skills when your muscles are tired is always good, as long as you don't push so hard that you get injured. Later you can add a player as a defender to pressure the player trapping the ball as she continues to receive passes on the ground and in the air.

Soccer was my first love . . .

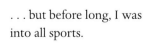

. . . but before long, I was into all sports.

Here I am with my copilot Garrett (smiling in foreground), enjoying the perks of being a military brat. Hey, what does this button do?.

Can you pick me out of the lineup? I'm in the front row on the far left. That's my dad, Bill, in the coach's shirt.

Even at fifteen, I knew where
I was heading . . . in this case,
for the national team.

I couldn't believe I was still in
high school, playing in the
Olympic Sports Festival with
UNC star Linda Hamilton (left)
and the great
Michelle Akers (right).

At Carolina, I never had to
apologize for my intensity.

Next to my family, Anson
Dorrance has been the most
influential person in my life.

◀ When I pulled on that jersey,
I felt we would never lose.

On the field, when you beat a player you've always got to be looking for the next option.

One of my best friends, Tisha Venturini, and I had a blast at UNC except when we looked like dorks posing for photo shoots.

Tiger Woods, you have nothing to worry about.

I took a day off from training to get married. My husband, Christiaan, is over my right shoulder. My mom is in a blue dress behind me and my dad is on the far left. I'd introduce the whole family, but we don't have enough room on the page.

I always say head coach
Tony DiCicco has four sons
and twenty-six daughters.

When we play with
Joy Fawcett's daughter,
Katie, our defense
eases up—a bit.

SEVEN

Passing

Making Your Teammates Look Good

When players are young, they want to dribble. And that's not necessarily a bad thing. Young players should be encouraged to dribble, to try different things, to be unafraid to fail. Creativity is an asset in soccer as in any endeavor, and of course, as dribbling is one skill that makes the U.S. Women's National Team the best in the world, we need more of those "personality players" who can slice through defenses once my teammates and I hang up our cleats.

But that said, we should never lose sight of how important passing is in soccer. In fact, good passing on a team can help you win and enjoy playing as much as or more than any other skill. A team that is able to string productive passes together will inevitably create scoring chances.

Fact: A team of poor passers can (and often does) win games by just booting the ball upfield as many times as possible. If they have some fast forwards, they will score some goals and win some games.

Fact: An average team that passes well will often beat a physically stronger opponent that doesn't.

Too often in this country, youth coaches sacrifice learning skills for winning games. Because speed and aggression are so important to winning soccer games, often coaches won't let their players take chances by passing the ball around a lot. The quicker you get the ball forward, the less likely it is that it will be stolen and lead to a quick counterattack. While valid, this shortsighted philosophy can be counterproductive

With numbers up you have a lot of options. Check out the backheel pass!

to developing athletes who can play the game with the same grace, skill, and power that has come to typify the U.S. Women's National Team.

When I was younger, I didn't pass as often as I probably should have. But as I grew older and evolved as a player, I saw the benefit of dishing the ball off to my teammates. Instead of having to dribble through a maze of slide-tackling defenders, I can pass, then sprint up the field and get the ball back. It's not as if I'm doing less work, but it's a lot more efficient—and a lot less painful!

As simple as it sounds, there are basically only two types of passes that require slightly altered technique. There is the short-to-medium pass, preferably on the ground, made with the inside or outside of your foot. And there's the long pass that has some air under it, most likely hit with the laces of your shoe.

There are three elements to the perfect pass: technique, pace, and accuracy. Concentrating on the correct technique—based on the type of pass you're making and the demands of the particular situation—will help you insure the other two.

No one can dribble through eleven players. As a matter of fact, I've found that no matter what eleven players come on the field to challenge you, scoring goals is never easy. Whether it is the 1995 Women's World Cup champion Norwegian National Team or a youth-club team, whether they be fast or slow, big or small, skillful or unskillful, those eleven players will always make life difficult for you as you get closer to the goal.

The amazing thing about passing is that players sometimes lose sight of the simple fact that with a crisp, accurate pass, you can cover more of the field than you can with even the best dribbling. Don't get me wrong; it's wonderful to have that dribbling mentality, and we shouldn't inhibit the excitement of "taking players on," but never forget that to pass is to move the ball much faster. Speed of play is so vitally important to unbalancing a defense and getting through to the goal. Slow passing means the defense has a chance to regroup and get organized. I like my defenses (for opponents, that is!) spread out and disorganized.

The ideal is to play the game in a one- and two-touch passing rhythm among your teammates, but of course that happens consistently only at the highest levels. In practice with the National Team, we often play with touch limitations—you can only touch the ball once or twice before you must pass—forcing us to play at a fast pace. The speed at which international soccer is played, the speed of players and the ball, will astound you if you've never seen it close up. If you ever have a chance to see an international game—women's or men's—from field level, you'll know what I mean. It will give you an even greater appreciation for the gifted athletes who play for their countries.

In games there is a time to pass and a time to dribble. Experience will dictate the appropriate action for each situation, and there is certainly no hard-and-fast rule. But in general, in the defense and midfield, provided you have an open teammate, a player should always look to pass first. A big exception to this is when you are squared up one-on-one with a defender in your attacking third or have no time or easy option to pass—then you just let your instincts take over and, hopefully, leave your opponent in the dust.

The reason passing should be your priority is that it creates one-on-one opportunities for dribbling (or, ideally, one-on-none for an open shot). Again, it's the quick movement of the ball among teammates that will stretch out and unbalance a defense, creating holes to be exploited by more passes or dribbles. Maintaining possession of the ball and passing forward, sideways, and backward with your teammates will always keep the defense on their heels. Your hope is that with a certain pass, you'll get a defender to move the wrong way, or pull her out of position to free up someone else. Usually you won't be able to crack any defense with one or two passes, or with only forward passes, so maintaining possession and passing backward and square are keys to eventually being able to rip a defense apart.

This leads us to choosing the best option for your pass, or to put it another way, deciding which pass will most benefit your team. Some players have great skills but constantly make bad decisions about where the ball should go and when. One key to choosing the right pass is reading the game before you get the ball, so when the ball does come to you you won't have to spend precious time deciding where to send it. You must always be aware of what's going on around you, always stealing a glance at the players moving around the field, while at the same time knowing where the ball is and keeping tabs on the defender marking you.

As you develop as a player, you will become more familiar with the flow and rhythm of the game, as well as your teammates, and you will be able to read the game more effectively. The most important key to reading the game is developing such a great comfort level with the ball that you can keep your eyes on the field instead of on your feet.

Trapping is a perfect example. You can't worry so much about the ball before it comes to you that you won't be able to see the game around you. And if an option that you wanted closes down as you get the ball, with your sharply

Julie reads the game on the fly.

refined skills and vision you'll be so good that you can take another option or make a new decision on the spot. This keeps the game moving at the high speed needed to produce winning, attacking soccer.

Of course, to exploit openings in a defense produced by good passing, you must have players who are fast enough and strong enough to take advantage of those opportunities, or your possession, while attractive, will not win games.

Conditioning yourself to make passing a priority is not easy. One aspect of my game that has evolved a lot since my college and early National Team career is my judgment in forgoing a shot in favor of passing to a person in a better position to score. I definitely made some "freshman mistakes" early on, taking unintelligent shots from bad angles.

One of the U.S. National Team's most impressive traits is

how well the players balance a killer instinct to score with an unselfishness in front of the net. It really is a unique part of our team. Now, if I happen to get endline on a defender, I am always looking for a teammate in a seam, and Tiffeny Milbrett and I have fed each other for goals many times in this situation. If I get around a defender and I have some time and space, I can shoot the ball from a poor angle and try to sneak it into the near post. The percentages say that it might go in, but the better choice is to pass it across the goal face to someone who could one-time it at a much larger target. To me, an assist is passing at the highest level. In 1998 I scored twenty goals for the National Team, but I also had twenty assists, and I recently became the career assist leader in National Team history. Soccer is a team game, and I take pride in setting up my teammates. I wouldn't have scored nearly as many goals if they weren't doing the same for me. I always make sure I thank or hug the person who gave me an assist on a goal because the point belongs to her as much as to me.

While you should never be afraid to pass back or square (the ideal is that the trapping skills of your teammates are such that you're never afraid to make a pass to them anywhere), your first option must always be to look forward. After all, the goal is forward, and that's where you want to go. But if that forward pass is not available, or "on," as we say, if there is no one open, please don't hit a LUB (long useless ball) to the forwards with only a fifty-fifty or less chance of their running it down! Instead, find an open player with a shorter forward pass, a square pass, or, if you have to, a back pass.

So many times players force bad passes to teammates who are tightly marked or to parts of the field that are congested. Of course, during games, you are constantly looking to make a penetrating pass that puts your teammates behind defenders, but if that pass is not on, you must find an open part of the field—the player under the least defensive pressure—and get her the ball. She will have the time to trap and choose the best option herself. If a team can get this rhythm—and trust me, it's not an easy thing to do—eventually that killer pass will be on, and if you have the skills to deliver that pass with the proper speed and accuracy, suddenly a teammate will be in position to score. That is the most exciting moment in a soccer game and one we all love to experience.

It was Julie Foudy who made perhaps the most important pass ever for women's soccer in the United States. As many of you may know, our Olympic semifinal match against our archrival, Norway, in the summer of 1996 in Athens, Georgia, went into sudden death overtime. There were 65,000 people in the stands screaming for us. In the one hundredth minute, Norway's goalkeeper, Bente Nordby, cleared a ball way over midfield. Joy Fawcett retreated and then attacked the ball to send a great header about 20 yards back up the field over a Norwegian defender. That's when Julie swooped in from the right flank, cleaned up the bouncing ball with a great trap on the run, took another touch as she ran at the defense, and then made history. Two defenders stepped toward Julie, and she slotted a perfect pass between them to Shannon MacMillan, who was making a run across the top of the penalty box toward the right side. Without breaking stride, Shannon shot the ball first time into the lower left corner from 12 yards out to end the game. The entire stadium went nuts. Her teammates went nuts. We were all so tired but so excited at the same time. We just made a huge dogpile on Shannon. It was unbelievable, a truly golden goal.

Shannon's goal sent us to the gold medal game and erased a year of frustration after losing to Norway in the semifinals of the 1995 Women's World Cup. The thing that was so great about Julie's pass was the pace, or as some coaches say, the "weight." The perfectly weighted pass allowed Shannon to one-touch the ball into the net. It's so tough for a goalkeeper to judge a shot if a player hits it first time. She can't cut down the angle and must rely on

"Golden Girl" Shannon MacMillan scored in
sudden-death overtime to put us in the
gold medal game of the 1996 Olympics.

reflexes alone to make the save. Shannon's finish was fantastic, but Julie had put the ball in exactly the right place. And this was in overtime after a tough 90-minute game. It just goes to show how important fitness is in executing your skills.

On the National Team, when the defenders and midfielders get the ball, one of the things they are looking to do is start our attacks as high, or as far downfield, as possible. We always try to get the ball forward because we want to start our attacking soccer as far into the other team's defense as possible. Whether the pass is coming from the goalkeeper, a defender, a midfielder, or even a forward, we want to possess the ball on the opponent's side of the field so if we do make a mistake and lose it, we still have some space to recover.

Sometimes that means the defenders are looking to serve all the way up to the attacking players, but most often they are looking to find our play-making midfielder, usually Julie or Michelle Akers, and they in turn will find an open player to keep the rhythm going. It is vitally important to playing attractive and winning soccer that your midfield dictate the tempo of the game. They receive the ball from one area, look forward, and if that pass is not on, they play to the opposite side or an area with the least amount of pressure.

But please don't lose sight of this: While we want to go forward quickly, we don't try to serve the farthest ball if it means that we will lose possession. Of course, the longer the pass, the less chance for accuracy, which is a fantastic reason to work on making your long passing dead-on. Possession is key. We want to keep the ball until we can go forward effectively. Sometimes we gamble and thump a long pass, but it must be a calculated risk. If the risk is too great, we will find another open player until the rhythm of the game dictates the best time to attack.

In the 1998 Goodwill Games in Long Island, New York, we were playing Denmark in our semifinal match of the four-team tournament. One of our outside defenders, Christie Pearce, had the ball on the left side of the field, just inside our own half, with no defensive pressure on her. Christie is very strong and delivers great long passes, and I remembered that she had hit some beautiful long balls in practice that week, so I took off running. Christie lofted a 40-yard pass with perfect pace and accuracy. I brought the ball under control in full stride, outmuscled a big Danish defender, rounded the sprawling goalkeeper, and slid the ball into an open net from 10 yards out. The goal, my third of the game, made it 5–0 and put us in the finals against China, which we won 2–0.

One pass, one goal. Not bad if you can pull it off, but against tough teams like Denmark, that's not going to happen very often. Conversely, the first goal of that match was entirely different. The attack started around our midfield when Julie received a pass from one of our defenders. She fed Kristine Lilly with a short pass in the center of the field about 35 yards from the goal. Kristine turned quickly with the ball and found me behind the defense on the left wing. I cut hard toward the goal and then, at the last possible moment, split two defenders with a square pass to Tiffeny Milbrett, who powered her shot past the Denmark goalkeeper from 10 yards out. Four passes made with weight and precision to break down a defense. Both goals were great sequences, and both showed how a team must be versatile in its passing, able to go forward, square, and back with equal efficiency.

Winning soccer games is also about risk: risking passes into tight space, risking your body to win a ball or dribble by a defender, and risking leaving holes in the defense or midfield by sending as many players as possible into the attack. In other words, risk is necessary to play winning and attractive soccer. But by developing your skills and keeping possession through passing, you can control the risk.

Please don't think that you should never pass to someone who is marked. Sometimes it's necessary, especially when you're playing great teams with strong defenses, or if you're trapped deep in your defensive third and looking to clear the ball out of danger. But if your passing skills are first-rate and the trapping skills of your teammates are also highly refined, you will always have passing options open to you. With more options, you can squeeze balls into tighter spaces to players moving at top speed or even to one with a big Danish defender on her back!

Brandi Chastain talked briefly in the last chapter about the importance of deception in soccer. This applies whether you are trapping, passing, dribbling, or shooting. If your opponent is surprised by your actions or not expecting a certain move, it will be all the more effective. This is especially true in passing, where sometimes all you need is a small space to fit a pass into or a defender moving the wrong way to allow one of your players to get open. As you become comfortable in your skills and master the ability to control the ball, you will be able to make deceptive passes that keep the defense guessing. You've seen many famous point guards in basketball make "no-look" passes on a fast break. Well, in soccer the best players also make those no-look passes because on the highest levels the defenders are tougher to fool and will intercept the telegraphed pass everytime. Soccer is a game of deception, and all great players share the ability to trick the defense into thinking they will pass one way with a quick glance or body movement.

I've often said that soccer is about numbers—getting more players into the attack than the other team has on defense, and getting more defenders back behind the ball than the other team has on the attack. By having numbers up on the other team, whether you are attacking or defending, you will always have an advantage.

This brings us to making runs for your teammates. As I said earlier, you must be willing to do the hard work—the running—to get numbers up on offense and defense for your team. Even if you have a team of great trappers and passers, if you are a stationary player and are not making runs for your teammates, they will be unable to pass effectively. Without productive passes, you will not be able to keep possession and advance up the field.

The goal is to keep the defense on the move and off balance, in order to create scoring opportunities. You should always be on the move after executing a pass. Stopping after a pass does your teammates no good and will allow your defender to expend little or no effort marking you. You always must be passing and moving to support the player with the ball, to get in position to receive a pass down the field, or to get back on defense if your team should lose the ball. Whether it leads to getting the ball directly or not, your movement, especially if it's dynamic, will force the defense to concentrate on containing you.

A dynamic run means one made at a sprint, showing a definite change of pace. Runs should be made at high speed, whether it's to support a teammate, to get behind a defense, or to run onto a through ball. It's about creating space—room for teammates to maneuver or lanes in which to pass.

If I'm close to a teammate who has the ball, I'm thinking about whether I need to support her by presenting myself for a pass or by clearing the area so she'll have room to operate. Maybe the space I'm in is the best place for her to dribble into, and I need to vacate that area pronto. Or, by giving her support, I may give her the option to pass to me to maintain possession or to play a quick give-and-go.

If I'm across the field from her and not in a position to give her direct support, I'm thinking about how my run can help the team in terms of maintaining possession or threatening the defense. I'm looking one, two, or three passes ahead and reading the flow of the game to try to get into a position where I can receive the ball and either take a shot or keep possession by passing or dribbling. Most of the time I don't get the ball, so I make another run, and another and another. It may seem like I'm just running, but every run I make is designed to pull a defender with me and maybe open up an option for another player. But beware: Don't run just for the sake of running, or you won't be able to last the whole game. Make your runs valuable to your team by putting yourself in position to receive the ball or opening space for your teammates.

Remember, to be effective, runs must be done at top speed with a change of pace, not only to lose defenders but to get those defenders to run with you. On the U.S.

National Team we take pride in our ability to possess the ball and play attractive soccer. Like all soccer players, we don't always perform well, but we are dedicated to producing entertaining and attacking soccer.

When people talk about the styles of the top soccer-playing nations, it seems that most of the description is based on how much emphasis these countries put on passing and how proficient they are.

Of the top women's soccer nations in the world, Norway more than all others plays a very direct style, generally bypassing their midfield in favor of long-passing to their forwards. Because most long balls are difficult to bring down cleanly, Norway's midfielders focus on winning the second ball, the ball that is cleared by the defense or won by the forwards. Then they attack from there. Norway does very well within its style. Each of its defenders can serve 40- to 45-yard passes that immediately put pressure on the opposition's defense. Norway's tall and athletic forwards win those air battles and are very good at combining passes in their attacking third to get behind the defense. They don't pass the ball around very much, but they're very effective nonetheless—and they win, a lot, including the Women's World Cup in 1995. They are a prime example of a team that hits long passes with precision and purpose. It's a very tough style to play against.

China has a style very similar to the USA's. The Chinese like to use their central midfielders as their playmakers. They are great passers, able to move the ball quickly and seamlessly. The midfielders look for slashing runs by forwards or a ball over the top on the opposite side to a flank midfielder. They really like to change the attack.

While Norway may be more predictable, China is very deceptive as a team. We must play organized defense to stop them, which we did in 1996 to win the Olympic Gold Medal by the slim margin of 2–1.

But when it comes to deception, Brazil is queen. The Brazilian women are starting to take on some of the qualities of their legendary men's teams. At times they seem to be trying to get as many people to touch the ball as possible. They move the ball around the field, looking for opportunities for their amazing dribblers to go at people one-on-one. If you aren't careful, you'll end up chasing them all over the field and tire yourself out. The Brazilians call it *ginga*, the ability to slip out of a tight space and fake defenders out of their shorts, and it's as much a signature of their game as the playground style is at the heart of American basketball. They don't want to just win, they want to do it in a spectacular fashion. They have advanced so much since the early 1990s that they shocked the world by finishing fourth at the 1996 Olympics, nearly upsetting China in the semifinal match. I know they will continue to improve and are wonderful role models when it comes to establishing rhythm in passing.

The style of the United States has changed a bit over the years. We are very offensive-minded but employ a variety of weapons in our attack. Sometimes we play through the midfield; other times we are more direct, opting to lob long balls directly from our defensive third deep into the opponent's backfield. Sometimes we'll flood one side with players and then switch the ball quickly to the opposite-side midfielder, an attacker, or even a defender going forward. Our versatility is definitely a strength, plus the fact that everyone on our team has the ability to be an attacking personality.

But whatever style your team plays, remember the basics of passing: technique, pace or weight, and accuracy. The perfect pass should be easy to trap and should enable your teammate to execute her best option. If you make a teammate look good, she will make you look good down the line.

Technique

If you can master the technique for both types of passing, you will be able to make any kind of pass in a game. Experience added to your technique will allow you to deliver sophisticated passes with small variations that go a long way toward making soccer a beautiful game to watch.

It is very important to remember that no two players are exactly the same and there is no *one* way to execute the skills of soccer. Each player will eventually develop her own style, which is part of the game's charm, but everyone should start off learning the same basic technique. And it all begins with a short pass.

I would call a short pass anything up to 20 yards, with a medium-range pass perhaps up to 30 yards, and these should be hit on the ground whenever possible. Every player loves receiving a well-struck pass that glides across a field like a cue ball on a pool table. Any pass over the 20- to 30-yard range will probably have to be in the air or the ball will almost surely be intercepted or deflected by the opposing team.

Whenever you make a pass, long or short, you must keep your ankle locked. If you are passing with the inside of your foot, you must make it a nice flat surface to the ball or the ball will spin where you don't want it to go. You must also make sure your toe is up (and locked) and that you follow straight through to your target, not across your body like I see so many young players doing.

Of course, if you are passing with the outside of your foot, your toe must be angled slightly down and, once again, locked. Often when you're passing with the outside of the foot there will be a bit of spin on the ball. As you develop better passing skills, you can use spin to your advantage and bend the ball to difficult-to-reach places on the field.

Passing with the inside of my foot.

This is not to say that you can't make a short pass with your instep or hit a long pass with the inside of your foot if you have the strength. But as a guiding rule, you will most often hit short passes with the inside or outside of your foot and long passes with your instep, especially if you drive a ball across the field.

The position of your plant foot, or nonkicking foot, is

also very important. It must never be too far in front, too far behind, or too far away from the ball. If it is, you will be off balance and increase the like-lihood of your pass missing the mark. In addition, you almost always want the toe on your plant foot to be pointed to where you want the ball to go, because the position of your foot will dictate how your hips swing through the ball, which is where the power comes from in kicking. If your toe is not pointed to where you want the ball to go, often your hip will swing toward that direc-tion and the pass will go astray.

Passing with the outside of my foot.

As you work on your passing, you will find the most comfortable position for your plant foot, and through much repetition you'll develop auto-matic muscle memory.

Long passing entails a slightly altered technique, although you are still following straight through and the position of your plant foot is similar. The majority of the time you will be making a long pass with your instep, or on your laces, slightly to the inside of your foot. You must still lock your ankle (do you see a recurring theme here?), but your toe will be pointed down so you can wedge your foot under the ball and get it up in the air. The distance is dictated by how much you get under the ball, where you hit it, and how hard you swing your leg. A feel for how to make a long pass will come in time, after many training sessions and games. Good skills don't come easily.

One more word about the plant foot on long passing. To get the ball up in the air, you must lean your body back a bit, and planting your foot just a tad behind the ball will

JULIE SAYS: After technique, the most important aspect of passing is putting texture on the ball. By texture—some call it weight—I mean the correct pace, spin, or loft, if needed. There are so many ways to put texture on the ball. You can spin it, float it

in so that it drops in behind the defense, drive it across the field to your teammate, or bend it into the corner of the net with finesse. It may require going on the ground, like my pass to Shannon in the Olympics, or giving it a little lift to get it over the foot of a defender. But recognizing what surface and what texture to put on the ball is an ability that all great passers have.

The Creator: Julie Foudy

Passing

help you do this. Of course, if you plant too *far* behind the ball (a common occurrence among young players), you will be reaching to kick and often get no power on the ball and little air, and of course an interception by the other team. If you plant too *close* to the ball or, worse, in front of it, you will jam yourself and won't be able to strike the ball in the best position to get it up in the air. That best position is an imaginary spot about halfway between the middle and the bottom of the ball. Practice hitting this spot with your laces, until the motion becomes second nature. You will eventually be able to hit long passes while standing or moving at top speed.

Hitting a long pass with the outside of your foot may be one of the toughest skills in soccer. It takes tremendous strength and great technique. Michelle Akers might be the best player in the world at hitting long passes with the outside of her feet. She can do it with both her left and right. As with anything, it requires practice, practice, practice. It may come slowly, but if you can master passes with all parts of your feet, a world of options will open up for you.

Julie Foudy has a terrific appreciation and feel for the little nuances you must acquire once you have mastered passing technique.

One more thing we must talk about—and this is getting a bit sophisticated—is *where* to pass to your player. Do you pass it right to her? Do you lead her so she runs into space? Of course, this is dictated by the flow of the game. If she is unmarked but has a defender about 10 yards from her, you pass it right to her feet. If there is space in front of her, lead her into that space, but remember, you must hit the pass with the proper speed and accuracy so she can run it down. How many times have you seen a soccer player hit a pass too hard? It happens all the time. This is why I often tell young players to just work on passing to a teammate's feet, to pass the ball straight to the target. If they try to lead a player, the ball will never reach a teammate. As they play more, a player will learn when to pass to feet and when to put the ball into space.

At the higher levels, you will eventually become so comfortable in your passing skills that you'll even pass to the foot, left or right, that your teammate prefers. Or you will pass to the foot that is the farthest away from the pressuring defender. If I'm checking and a defender is on my left side, I want the ball passed to my right foot. I can then control the ball with either foot and keep it away from the defender. A well-placed pass by my teammate makes this a lot easier.

Passing Games/Drills

Keys to remember:
- Lock the ankle.
- Short passing: Contact the ball with the inside of the foot and toe up, or with the outside of the foot with the toe down.
- Long passing: Keep the toe down, wedged under the ball.
- Keep the plant foot pointed to target.
- Follow through toward the target with kicking foot.
- Use both the inside and outside of feet.
- Accuracy: Pass the ball to a teammate in the spot that makes it as easy as possible for her to trap.

- Pace: Pass fast enough to get the ball to target but not so fast as to make it difficult to trap.

The Wall

Yes, the wall again. A wall is great because you don't need a partner, there is no one to get mad at you if your passes don't hit the target, and no one has to run the balls down. With a wall, you can practice using all surfaces of your feet and developing good balance and technique. As you practice, your technique will evolve so that you are hitting crisp passes and well-driven balls. The wall is best for short passing, unless in a rare instance you have a lot of space. Once again, you can practice chipping balls and bending balls, and most of the time, if you hit a good pass with good technique, pace, and accuracy, it will come right back at you so you can practice your trapping and then move on to the next kick. I love a good wall.

Pairs Passing

Again, we're staying simple here, because that is the best way to learn and improve. Begin by passing the ball with your partner about 10 yards away. Slowly increase the distance as you get more comfortable. Use both feet and try all surfaces. Start basically static, then increase your movement until every pass and trap is made on the run. As you get more advanced, do this drill in a two-touch rhythm, where your first touch is a trap that prepares the ball to be passed and the second touch is the pass, short, medium, or long. This drill serves you well to sharpen your skills and to warm up before a practice or a game. Of course, it also helps with your trapping. Remember, do this drill at pace. Challenge yourself!

Five versus Two

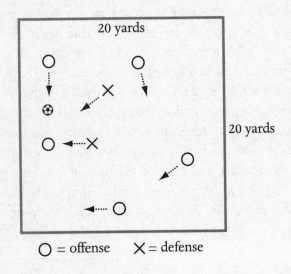

FIVE VERSUS TWO

Everyone has played Five versus Two, and it's a great drill for mastering passing. This is basically just a keep-away game with the five players on the outside (I don't want to call it a circle because the shape is always changing) keeping the ball away from two defenders in the middle. The player who gives the ball away goes into the middle, with the player who's been in the middle the longest going to the outside. The best grid size is 15 × 15 yards or 20 × 20 yards, and while the players should attempt to keep the drill in a confined space, it will morph around like an amoeba at times, especially with young players, which is okay as long as the players are conscious of regaining the shape as they play. It's not fair to the players in the middle to be too spread out, nor does it realistically reflect game action. With top players, you will be able to keep the drill in a very small space and still perform it productively. Players must move with and without the ball, constantly supporting one another and opening up new angles to receive a pass. The goal of the drill is to string as many passes together as possible. If you can keep the ball until the defenders are too tired to run anymore, you've got *ginga* in your game! But if you can consistently connect ten or more passes without losing the ball or a defender intercepting, you are still doing the drill well.

Ideally, when you get to the top level, Five versus Two is played with only one-touch passing. I wasn't good at this drill for a long time because it requires really sharp technique to come through in a small space. You have to be extremely accurate, and the pace of your passes must be exactly right because your teammates have very little time to receive the ball and make their next pass. You always have to be reading ahead to decide on your next pass. I really struggled with this! But as I came to understand that Five versus Two is basically a real soccer game without the shooting, I focused on getting better at it. You can split defenders, throw a quick dribbling move, and hit short and long passes. You are always supporting your players and constantly moving to receive passes. Sounds like a soccer game to me!

5 Passes = 1 Goal

This drill brings Five versus Two to the next level, with more space and more players. You can play with four to eight players on two teams of equal strength. If you have eight players, your grid size can be midfield to the top of the penalty box extended to the sideline. Five passes connected equals a goal, but once you get five, you keep going, and if you can get another five, and another, you compile more goals. Once again, players should always be moving and supporting their passes as well as concentrating on passing with pace and accuracy. In this drill you can also work on long passes as you look to switch the ball to open space on the field.

EIGHT

Dribbling

Take on Your Opponent

ribbling is a skill that can bring a stadium full of people to their feet, mold legends, and produce singular moments of greatness that stand forever in the minds of those who witness them. What could be more fun?

Many people have said that my dribbling, my one-on-one ability, is what makes me a special player. I do take pride in this skill, which like many parts of soccer is as mental as it is physical. But while many say that great dribblers are born and not made, dribbling is a skill that can be practiced, refined, and improved.

THE ANATOMY OF A JUKE   1. I set up the defender.

3. So I cut the ball back . . .

2. She's leaning the wrong way.

4. . . . and try to explode into that first step.

5. The ball is by her and she's beaten.

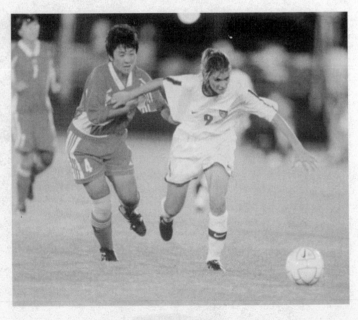

7. . . . or take me down.

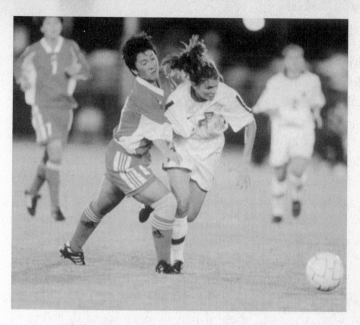

6. Now, she can either concede the breakaway . . .

8. Hey, ref, blow the whistle already!

It is important to note that to be a consistently effective dribbler, you must possess speed and strength. You can fake a defender out of her cleats, but if you don't have the speed and strength to take advantage of the space you have created, she can recover and get back in your way. If you can't free yourself from defenders, it will be difficult to get into position to take a solid shot. There are many ways they'll try to slow you down: They'll jam their shoulder into you, hook your arm and ride you off the ball, or simply knock you off your feet. But putting these tenacious defenders behind you is what creates havoc in an opponent's defense.

I like to break dribbling down into three types, which require slightly different techniques. There is open-field dribbling, shield dribbling, and of course, what everyone thinks of when they talk about dribbling: one-on-one dribbling—beating players with jukes and speed. This is one of the most exciting parts of soccer and puts the high beam on those who excel at it. Fans love these wizards with the ball, and every great team has at least one. Because we are fortunate enough to field several, the U.S. Women's National Team has been the dominant force in women's soccer this decade.

And remember this: To consistently win soccer games, sooner or later someone is going to have to put a defender behind her, whether it's through quick combinations of passes or through one-on-one dribbling.

When you beat a player, and I mean showing her your jersey number by blowing past and leaving her in the dust, another defender must come to cover and try to slow you down. This opens up space in the defense, perhaps leaves another player open, and then fun things start happening in the opponent's penalty box. Think of the danger you're creating if you beat more than one player and take several defenders out of the play! Suddenly you are numbers up in your attacking third and teammates are making the runs for you in the penalty box.

Good dribbling is a lot more than a couple of flashy moves. As I said, it takes speed and strength, but also bravery. You must have mental toughness to challenge players one-on-one. You must be willing to put your body on the line, because all too often when you burst past a player, you come down in a heap of tangled legs and pulled jerseys and get a face full of grass. It takes courage to keep running at the same defender time and again or to weave through a midfield packed with players kicking at your shins, knees, and sometimes thighs.

One of my best dribbling runs ever came against England at Spartan Stadium in San Jose, California, in 1997. There were more than 17,000 people in the stands, and the U.S. team gave them a great show, winning 5–0.

The play started on an England corner kick that was punched away by our goalkeeper, Tracy Ducar, and then cleared out of our defensive third by Lorrie Fair. The ball fell to Tiffeny Milbrett about 20 yards inside our half, and she took off like the human bullet that she is. At about midfield, she passed to me on the left flank. Since it was such a quick counterattack, I found myself looking at about 45 yards of green grass and the goal. I collected the ball in full flight and streaked toward the goal, but an English defender was tracking back fast and running with me. As I neared the top of the penalty box, I cut the ball hard to the inside because the defender was sprinting and I thought I could use her momentum against her. But as I cut inside, she slowed down and I didn't have room for a shot. So as she tried to recover inside, I cut the ball back to my left, took a touch, and shot with my left foot from a tight angle, about 7 yards away from the goal. It was two razor-sharp cuts done in perfect rhythm that spun the defender in a full circle. I was just trying to get the ball on the face of the goal, but my shot went straight into the upper-right corner. The stadium erupted, and I took off running toward the sideline before being engulfed by my teammates. It was a truly great moment, because it showed how exciting and dynamic women's soccer can be.

As I look back on that play, it's easy to dissect it, but while it was happening I wasn't thinking, I was just acting. And that's dribbling. In games you don't have time to think, "Well, I'm going to do this move here, then that move, and then shoot." The game happens too fast. That's why the best dribbling practice is to play games and never be afraid to try to dribble past defenders. Once you master some basic moves and work on them over and over in practice, the more often you'll find yourself using them in games and the more effective they will be.

As I said in the previous chapter, young players should never be discouraged from dribbling. Of course, there is a time to dribble and a time to pass, and you must learn the difference, because you don't want players dribbling in their defensive third or dribbling when there are open players. Nonetheless, as a young player you *should* take a chance, knowing you will sometimes lose the ball but also that expressing yourself with the ball is the only way to learn.

Pickup games are where some of the great dribblers are developed. In Brazil, which produces the best dribblers in the world, players hone their moves in the streets of Rio de

Janeiro and São Paulo. There are no coaches or parents in the streets and parks screaming, "Pass the ball!" There is just a bunch of kids running around, juking each other, trying fancy ball tricks and having a great time. "Watch me! I'm Ronaldo!" they cry, imitating one of their idols. And when they get in real game situations, they aren't afraid to try to make a little magic. We must instill this mentality in our young players. If they are not going to play pickup with their friends—and it's a major problem that in our country so few young players do—then they must be encouraged to be creative in practice.

You've heard some players get called "ball hog," but the fact is that in practice everyone should take a turn being a ball hog sometimes. This is how you learn to dribble, by practicing when it doesn't matter how many times you lose the ball.

Young players should be encouraged to dribble. But keep that head up!

There is nothing wrong with trying moves over and over during practices and scrimmages, as long as you understand when to dribble and when to pass once you step into a game.

In practice you should play dribbling games, challenge each other and have fun doing it. This way, knowing that in competitive games you can't dribble all the time, that you must pick your openings to take someone on, you'll be that much more likely to succeed when the opening comes.

But what is the best time to dribble?

Put simply, there are three situations in a game where you should choose to dribble rather than pass. First, when there is open space in front of you. Second, when you are squared up one-on-one with a defender in your attacking half of the field. Third, when the options are limited in the midfield and you need to maintain possession.

Good midfielders must be able to slip tackles, put defenders behind them, and connect with other midfielders and forwards, or if necessary, advance the ball alone and shoot. Midfielders with this ability are absolutely vital in maintaining possession for your team and generating an effective attack.

One-on-one opportunities are your chance to put your individual stamp on the game. When you get a player isolated anywhere in the attacking third, take her on, with the goal of either serving the ball into the penalty area or shooting yourself. I like to think that only good things can happen if you continually challenge players on the flanks. Yes, sometimes you will get stuffed and the other team will be off on the attack. But if you are trying to dribble in your attacking third and the opponent gains possession far from your goal, there should be defenders behind you to cover.

Take the risk! More often than not, dribbling at a player in the corner will result in a cross, your getting fouled, or, at the worst, forcing a corner kick. Not a bad worst option!

In short, I encourage you to take players on. Aggressiveness is a characteristic of the American female player that we need to continue to cultivate. The world knows the U.S. team has great one-on-one artists, and you could be the next one!

We've talked about how soccer is a game of deception, and dribbling—getting a defender to think that you'll do one thing with the ball when you're about to do another—is the ultimate deception.

There are many different dribbling moves you can master. Of course, the ultimate weapon is speed, to just push the ball past a player and run by her. Joy Fawcett is speed incarnate. She played midfield for the National Team early in her career, and just a tap on the brakes was enough for Joy to lull defenders and blow past them on the flanks. She would slow down just enough to coax the defender into easing up, then she'd push it and go. When she gets some space on the wing, she can do some serious damage. We all saw that in the 1996 Olympics final when she streaked down the right side to set up Tiffeny Milbrett for the winning goal.

If you have tremendous speed, you will need fewer moves, but as you advance to higher levels, the players get faster and stronger and speed alone will not cut it. You must have some guile. You must get a defender off balance or leaning the wrong way. Sometimes a slight movement—a sway of the body, a dart of the eyes—is all it takes to get a defender to commit. In that split second where her weight is going the wrong way, you slash past her in the other direction.

One person who had a big influence on my dribbling when I joined the National Team was Carin Gabarra. Carin was voted MVP of the 1991 FIFA Women's World Cup, and for good reason. She was unstoppable and her three goals in our 5–2 semifinal victory over Germany stand together as one of the single greatest performances ever. Carin was part of our devastating forward line—along with April Heinrichs and center forward Michelle Akers—at the first Women's World Cup in China (I played midfield then). Dubbed the "Triple-Edged Sword" by the media, this trio could slice open defenses with lethal dribbling runs.

Carin, who played her last match for the USA in the 1996 Olympics Gold Medal game, could basically screw a defender into the ground with her razor-sharp cuts. Part of her secret was that she is slightly pigeon-toed, and that allowed her to make cuts that were so radical they were almost backward! Okay, they only *looked* like she was going backward, but that was because the opponents were so off balance and Carin got so much separation from her defender that she was able to penetrate with startling quickness. She would do one cut after another, and in her prime she was truly one of the greatest dribblers in the world, earning her the nickname Crazy Legs. It fit, because those legs were going everywhere, as were the defenders. I remember just watching her burn defenders and spin them around; they would literally fall over backward trying to stay with her!

Currently, one of our best and most exciting dribblers is Tiffeny Milbrett. Tiffeny is small, at 5 feet 2 inches (she claims 5 feet 3 inches!), but she's blazingly fast and tremendously strong for her diminutive frame. She has a break-neck dribbling style, or what coaches call pure technical speed. She just runs right at you, dares you to step toward her, to dive in, and then *whoosh*, she's gone. It's absolutely amazing how she can dribble at top speed. One of the things that makes Tiffeny so dangerous is that she runs at pretty much the same pace with the ball as without. Sometimes it seems like she's out of control and that she's touched the ball too far out in front of her, but I guess

Against China in the 1995 Women's World Cup, Carin Gabarra shakes two defenders with one of her trademark cuts.

that's why she makes defenders look foolish—when they lunge for the ball, she beats them to the spot and slashes past them. Even when her cuts aren't dramatic, she is either going so fast or her first step is so explosive that the defender has little more than a prayer.

Tiffeny's dribbling sometimes reminds me of the great Diego Maradona of Argentina, who in his prime was able to work his way out of tight spaces and beat players with apparent ease in the open field. At the 1986 World Cup in Mexico, he dribbled through what seemed like the entire English defense by himself. It was probably one of the most dazzling individual efforts in the history of soccer. He collected the ball at midfield and sliced through about six players, *dribbled* past the goalkeeper, and scored! What was so impressive about Diego's run was that even though he

TIFFENY SAYS: My dribbling style is kind of like that of a racehorse waiting at the gate to be released. When that gate opens, in other words, when I see an opening in the defense, I'm off to the races. I guess I developed my dribbling style when I was young and I only wanted to score goals. Because I was faster than most kids, I always went straight to the goal and was rarely stopped. Now, at the highest levels, you pick and choose your spots. You learn when you can dribble and when you can't. International soccer demands that you make those decisions. As a youth player, you can take more risks and develop as a player. Coaches should give their players the green light to take people on in the right situation. Luckily, I've always had that freedom. If was moving at high speed, it looked like the ball was attached to his laces at all times. That's mastery.

Now, I know I've put a lot of emphasis on speed in dribbling, but you don't have to be superfast to be a productive dribbler. Tisha Venturini isn't the fastest, but she makes up for it with tremendous skill. Tisha's dribbling style features fakes, windups, quick cuts, and misdirections. Given the chance, Tisha will hat a defender by flipping the ball over her opponent's head, dragging it with the sole of her foot, pushing it through their legs for a nutmeg, or stepping one way and cutting it another. Smooth with the ball, she always seems to be able to shake free of a defender in a tight space, make a productive pass, or take a crisp shot. University of North Carolina head coach Anson Dorrance once said that Tisha could dribble by people in a phone booth. That's how

you lose the ball, you lose it. As a forward, you expect to lose the ball a few times. No one can score a goal every time she gets the ball (not even Mia!), but that once or twice in a game when you do beat a player or two, you can create brilliance.

The Human Bullet: Tiffeny Milbrett

compact and controlled her touches are. Her technique is very clean, and her feet are lightning quick. While Tiffeny emphasizes her speed, Tisha relies on deception.

Michelle Akers has a dribbling style all her own. I don't know if there has ever been a female player who combined such power and grace. Michelle is so strong that when she has the ball, it's tough for defenders to get close. She keeps them at a distance with her arms and body, and at times she thunders straight through them. She combines this raw strength with finesse and epitomizes adaptability. She played forward until 1996 and was almost impossible to stop once running at goal. Now as a center midfielder she strides around the field and has the superior skills to dribble out of trouble and keep possession for our team.

Kristine Lilly and I are slashing-type dribblers. We like to use change of pace and a lot of stop-and-go moves. We've been blessed with a quick first step and the ability to stop and start with precision. I also believe I've developed a dribbler's mentality over the years, as I relish the opportunity to take on a defender when I get squared up in the offensive third. All great dribblers have this mind-set.

Another characteristic of the best dribblers is their ability to hold the ball under pressure, or shield dribble. Shield dribbling is perhaps the most ignored skill in soccer but, ironically, one of the most important. How many times in a game do you get the ball and have no passing option? At these times you must be able to hold the ball while working yourself free to pass or shoot. Often you are in tight space with a player either hanging on your back or chasing you at close range.

Despite her lack of size, Tiffeny is awesome at holding the ball. She keeps her center of gravity low and her body between the defender and the ball while she pivots and weaves to create space. You often have to hold a player off with your arms and body while keeping the ball moving so the defender never has a window to steal it. But you can't be afraid to take a few hits from behind. This is one situation where the hands and arms actually come into play. You are always using them for balance, but when shield dribbling you also use them to fend off the player marking you.

As I've said, soccer is a physical game, and it entails a great amount of grabbing, pushing, and shoving. The trick is to fight through the melee and emerge with the ball.

Dribbling in a tight space is not one of my strengths, but I've worked hard to improve. I'm much better with room to run at the defender. Brandi Chastain and Tisha, however, thrive when cornered. They are equally adept with the insides and outsides of both feet and, when shielding the ball, will often use the soles of their cleats to maintain contact with and manipulate the ball. This allows them to keep possession while looking to pass or work themselves free.

The third type of dribbling takes place in the open field. There are times in the game when you have acres

When shielding, always keep your body between the defender and the ball.

of territory ahead of you and must exploit them quickly or watch them disappear. When dribbling in the open field, you must take longer touches, keep your head up so you can read your options, and dribble the ball into the most dangerous area before taking a shot or making an incisive pass. You should be at top speed in the open field, unlike in one-on-one dribbling where you are constantly changing gears.

So many players get behind a defender on the flank and burst into open space, only to take a hard touch toward the corner flag instead of cutting toward the goal. When you get past that defender and the sweeper is too far away to cover, you *must* take your first touch at an angle toward goal. Be brave and slot your body in front of the defender. If she takes you down, it might be a yellow card or a red card and certainly will give your team a good chance to send a free kick into the box or, if you're already in the penalty area, result in a P.K. If the defender doesn't foul you, the goalkeeper will have to rush toward you, narrowing the angle and giving you options for a shot or a pass to the back post.

This brings us to one of the most important points of this chapter. Dribbling is only productive if it ends with a pass or a shot. If you dribble all over the field and beat all ten players only to lose the ball, what have you accomplished? Even Maradona's historic run wouldn't be remembered if the ball hadn't ended up in the back of the net.

In October 1997 we played two matches in Germany; we lost the first one 3–1, in driving rain. Germany is one of the best teams in the world, and they really put on a clinic in that first game. Three days later we played a great all-around game and won 3–0. In that match Tiffeny Milbrett had several of her spectacular solo dribbling runs. With about fifteen

Skinning two Swedish defenders in the 1996 Olympics.

minutes left in the first half and the game tied 0–0, she created the first goal when she collected a ball 40 yards from the net and ran at the German midfield. On a full sprint, she slashed past two defenders before threading a pass to me at the top of the penalty box. I sidestepped one defender to the inside, took a hard stride to goal, and rolled a left-footed shot into the left corner of the net from 10 yards out.

Tiffeny's dribbling was productive because she found a teammate at the end of the run and we scored a big goal. Passing off the dribble, especially when you are going at high speed, is one of most difficult parts of soccer. It's very tough to read the game when you're trying to avoid slide tackles and maintain control of the ball at high speeds.

Now, dribbling is not just for midfielders and forwards.

Take on Your Opponent

Defenders dribble too, although it is unwise to dribble in your defensive third unless you absolutely have to. However, they can and should push forward into midfield and their attacking third, and therefore they must be adept at this skill. The modern defender doesn't just tackle hard and win balls in the air. She has to able to play with the ball at her feet, take advantage of open space in front of her, and yes, if the situation dictates, have the ability to dribble by a few players.

Make no mistake, dribbling carries risk because the ball is at your feet for an extended period of time and the ball is what the opponent wants. They will do pretty much anything to get it. This is why you must always keep your head up and be aware of your surroundings. Dribbling so fast that you can't make decisions with the ball is not productive. If someone tries to tackle you, you should always be able to pass, shoot, make a quick move, or, at worst, jump out of the way. Great dribblers are always on the edge of being out of control but rarely are.

If you do get taken down, and it happens all the time, never let the defender think she has rattled you, which is often her goal. Just get up and play. Hopefully, if it's a foul, the referee will protect you by cautioning the player and, if the fouling persists, red-card her. Either way, you must always take the high road. Don't retaliate. Let *them* get the card.

I know from experience that it's tough to keep your cool, and sometimes even I have trouble staying under control when I'm on the receiving end of a particularly harsh tackle. Mind you, I pride myself on controlling my temper on the field. If you don't, it's sure to get the best of you eventually. It will never benefit your team to lash back. You're liable to get tossed, and your team will suffer for it.

Technique

As with all soccer skills, to become a good dribbler you must become very comfortable with the ball at your feet. You must be able to dribble with all the surfaces of your feet—inside and outside, soles and laces.

Remember, your ankle must be locked whenever contacting the ball, but in dribbling the technique is not quite the same as in trapping or passing. Your ankles have to be supple and able to change position constantly. The touch on the ball, this suppleness, can only be achieved with much ball work, which includes juggling as well as repetitively practicing on individual dribbling moves.

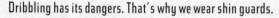

Dribbling has its dangers. That's why we wear shin guards.

It is important to always be light on your feet while dribbling. By this I mean that your feet are always moving as you cut and fake. If you are planted into the ground, it will be very tough to dribble effectively. You must learn how to shift your weight from foot to foot to be as dangerous a dribbler as possible.

Some dribblers rely mostly on cutting the ball, others like to pull and push the ball with the soles of their cleats, and still others like to use a variety of fakes or a combination of the three. To become a good dribbler, you really only need to master these basics. Once they become second nature, you can experiment with fancier moves, perhaps nutmeg a few players, hat someone, or pull off some unbelievable trick you didn't know you had in you.

By basic moves, I mean the most common ones players use to change direction with the ball. You can work on these by yourself or in pairs during practice. The most important and effective move you must master is cutting the ball with the inside and outside of your feet. Later you'll learn to pull and push with the soles of your cleats, as well as several feints like passing your foot over the ball to move it to the inside

The object of the stepover is to get your opponent leaning one way . . .

of your body or toward the outside, often called the step-over and the scissors, respectively.

All of these moves become more effective when you combine them with windups, meaning faking a shot or a pass in hopes of freezing a defender or making her step the wrong way. Then you execute a cut or pull the ball in the direction you want to go, leaving her on her heels or, better, on the ground. Rapidly changing pace works just as well to throw your defender off balance and open up an avenue for you to advance, which, after all, is the essence of dribbling.

Most people prefer to dribble primarily with their strong foot (Maradona used his left foot almost exclusively), and while you certainly can be an effective dribbler this way, it's

... and then to take the ball in the other direction.

best to use both feet with equal proficiency. The value of using both feet cannot be understated, as you'll soon see. Always practice your dribbling with both. If you practice a move ten times with your strong foot, do it fifteen times with your weak one. You may not be as smooth with your off foot, but dogged practice leads to the ultimate praise: "Is she right-footed or left-footed?"

Always keep the ball close to your body, or else you risk a defender poking it away or, worse, you end up on the losing end of a hard slide tackle. To keep the ball close, you must dribble with the inside, outside, and laces of your foot. The outside of the foot is often best because it keeps the ball close and allows you to maintain your natural stride. When dribbling in the open field, you want to use the outside of your foot almost exclusively.

As you become more comfortable on the ball, you will start to develop the ability to read the game as you dribble. Vision is essential if you plan to connect with productive passes or jump on opportunities for shots as they arise. This is what you strive for, dribbling by feel, with only short glances at the ball, like Maradona with the ball attached to his laces.

Many times the best way to keep a defender from dispossessing you is to keep your body between her and the ball. This is especially true in shield dribbling, but it holds for one-on-one dribbling as well. As you dribble by a player, if she is on your left side, it makes sense to keep the ball on your right foot. If the ball is on your closest foot to the defender, even if she is off balance, flat-footed, or essentially beaten, a last stab of her toe might poke the ball away. Not so if the ball is on the opposite foot from the defender. Then you are usually past her and onto the next challenge.

This is why it is so important to be proficient with both feet. The best dribblers can go to their left or right and if a defender shades one way or the other, they always have options. If a defender knows that you can only dribble with your right foot, you will be much easier to defend.

Dribbling can be one of the most electrifying parts of soccer for you and the fans. As you develop your own style, take pride in your ability to beat people. Play boldly, always experimenting, and never be satisfied.

Dribbling Games/Drills

Keys to remember:

One-on-one dribbling:

- Keep the ball close to your body.
- Keep your head up.
- Dribble with the inside and outside of your feet.

Open-space dribbling:

- Keep the ball close to your body so defenders can't get it but far enough in front so you can run at speed and change direction.
- Keep your head up.
- Use primarily laces and the outside of your foot.

Shield dribbling:

- Keep the ball close to your body.
- Keep your body between the defender and the ball.
- Use both the inside and outside of your feet.
- Always be looking to pass or shoot.

Repetition of Basic Moves

One great thing about dribbling is that you can do a lot of training on your own with an eye toward developing that relationship, that *feel*, for the ball. There are many moves that you can practice, but it is best to start with the basics; once you have them mastered, the fancy stuff will follow.

Dribble several yards, then cut and change direction with the inside of your right foot. Do it ten times, then switch to the outside of your right foot. Do several sets with your left foot. You should work on pullbacks—dribble, then step on the ball and pull it back in the opposite direction with enough pace so that you can break into a run. You can then work on your stepovers, stepping all the way over the ball and then dribbling back in the opposite direction. If you step over the ball from the inside to the outside, then take the ball back to the inside with the inside of your foot; we call that a scissors move. If you do it from the outside to the inside, and then take the ball back outside with the outside of your foot, you've done what we call a basic stepover.

Another classic is the stutter step—where you slow your pace with a series of light touches on the inside of your foot—the stutter—luring the defender in tight, where she will have to shade you one way or the other, and then cutting the ball back the other way with the outside of your foot. The idea is to coax her to lean in the direction of your stutter and then blow past the other way, while she is off balance. If you can master this move with both feet, you will be especially dangerous.

Once you become comfortable, you can combine all

these moves and have a small arsenal of dribbling tricks on which to build—and maybe a scholarship, to boot.

Often when I train on my own, I set up a number of cones in a line and weave in and out of them. You see teams and players doing this all the time, but it will not be very beneficial unless you push yourself by constantly increasing your speed. As I mentioned before, the best dribblers are always on the verge of losing control. Another way to challenge yourself is to move the cones closer together. The goal of this drill is to develop quick feet and to be able to change direction with the ball in tight spaces. As difficult as it can be, this drill is not very realistic to game situations, but in the absence of another player to practice with, it's helpful for perfecting technique. Be sure to use the inside and outside of both feet. You may want to do one set with the inside or outside of the right foot, then switch to the left on the way back. Never shortchange yourself by doing fewer repetitions with your off foot. The best players consciously do more with their weak foot.

One-on-One

Playing one-on-one with a friend is a fantastic way to develop your dribbling skills. One game is to place two cones about 10 yards apart, with the area in between serving as a kind of goal. The objective is to beat your opponent and dribble between the cones for a point. If you have several players, you can alternate trying to beat the defender through the cones, rotating defenders after everyone has taken a designated number of turns. You can also play with small goals in a 10 × 15-yard grid and dribble at each other over and over. This game is very fatiguing but a marvelous way to work on not only your dribbling skills but your fitness as well. You can try all sorts of moves, from the basic to the showboating, and finish it off with a shot. Cindy Parlow, a brilliant one-on-one player with a great future at the international level, credits extra time spent dueling her friends (guys, in this case) as a major reason for her success as one of college soccer's premier strikers in recent years.

Small-Side Games with Touch Restrictions

Ideally, you should play five on five in about a 40 × 50-yard grid, which gives you enough space to dribble freely but not too many passing options. This is basically a game of keep-away, except that each player *must* take at least four touches or beat another player before she can pass. Remember, it doesn't matter how many people you beat unless your dribbling ends in a pass or shot.

Steal the Bacon

There aren't many games more fun than Steal the Bacon. Split the team in half with an even number of players in a line on either side of the goal and a goalkeeper in the nets. Each player has a partner on the other team who she will go against, and they are both assigned identical numbers. Therefore, you have two 1's, two 2's, two 3's, and so on. The coach or a server has all the balls about 40 yards from the goal. The coach calls out a number and then puts a ball in play to a random part of the field. The players whose numbers were

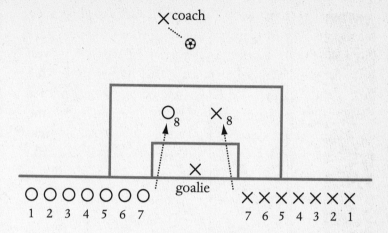

STEAL THE BACON

called sprint for the ball, and whoever wins it tries to dribble past her opponent and score. If the other player steals the ball, she becomes the offensive player and you the defender. The competition continues until someone shoots or the coach decides that the two have been going at it long enough and calls a new number. By calling up to four numbers at the same time, you can create a four-on-four game. The first team to make ten goals wins.

A variation is allowing your teammates who are standing on the goal line outside the post to be used as passing options—but they can only have one touch and have to stay behind the end line. Stay alert! Sometimes shots go wide and you can one-touch it back into the field of play to your teammate. This is a terrific way to test your one-on-one dribbling and your shooting, as well as your defense.

NINE

Shooting

Be a Finisher

've taken thousands of shots in my soccer career. Thousands of shots on my own, in practices, and in games. And when I was a young player, most of them didn't go in the goal. Today a lot of them still don't go in. But that has never stopped me from shooting whenever I get the chance. No matter how many balls flew over the crossbar or were saved by the goalkeeper, I just kept shooting. I learned a long time ago that there is something worse than missing the goal, and that's not pulling the trigger.

But if shooting and scoring were easy, it wouldn't be such a special thing to "put the biscuit in the basket." The great goal scorers of the world are idolized and worshipped—and, yes, paid the most money. They are that rare breed of player who can make the difference between winning and losing. To be a great goal scorer, you must have a burning desire to put the ball in the back of the net and shoot whenever you get the chance.

Another important element of shooting is kicking the ball so that it's directed somewhere on the frame of the goal. No shot in history has gone into the goal if it was flying over the crossbar. But if you put your shot on frame, the ball could ricochet off someone's leg, hit a bump in front of the goal-keeper, skid in off the wet ground, or fly by the goalkeeper because her vision was blocked.

I remember a game we played against Australia before the Olympics. One of our players took a seemingly harm-less shot that was bouncing slowly toward the goal. The

I caught this volley pretty good. I hope I didn't break the camera.

Australian goalkeeper thought it was going wide of the net, so she kind of relaxed, but I guess the ball hit a bump on the field or something because, much to her horror, it slipped into the corner of the goal and we won 2–1. That should be a lesson to all you shooters: You never know where that ball will end up until you shoot it.

Too often players try to blast every shot as hard as they can. Don't get me wrong; you should strike every shot with good pace, but the primary focus should be putting your shots inside the frame of the goal. If you try to kill the ball, more often than not you'll send it soaring over the goal.

The space in which you have to score may look big, but it's not. It's only about 8 feet high and 24 feet wide, and those pesky goalkeepers do a good job of making that space seem even smaller. This is why I always stress that if you keep the ball on the face of the goal, even if the shot is at the goalkeeper, at least you have a chance of it possibly going in. But if you miss your shot wide or high, you'll never know what wonderful things could have happened had that ball been on goal.

The third thing to remember when shooting is to keep the ball low. Besides eliminating the possibility of skying your shot, it's tough for goalkeepers to get down to the ground quickly to make a save. A keeper can only get down to the ground as fast as gravity will allow, but her hands are already up in the air and prepared to save shots that are headed for her midsection or higher.

I've heard coaches say that only one of every ten shots taken will go into the net. While no one knows the real percentage (and it's probably less than that), let's consider one out of ten as an example. If you can increase your per-

The position of your plant foot is critical to your success in shooting.

centage to just two out of ten, after one hundred shots you will have twenty goals, and in a sport where one goal often wins a game, that ten-goal difference is huge.

So how do you increase your percentage? Technique. By evolving from being just a shooter to become a finisher, someone who finishes her chances to score in any number of different and creative ways, always taking into account the exact shot that will get the job done. Often you don't need to hit the ball as hard as you can to score a goal. One situation may call for a 25-yard blast, while another may simply require tapping the ball into the net. The true finishers determine which surface of their foot to use and which type of shot to take based upon the situation in the game.

In fact, you can increase your scoring percentage when you take several factors into consideration: (1) where you are on the field; (2) the angle that you are shooting from; (3) where the defenders are; (4) where the goalkeeper is; and (5) what surface of your foot or body to use.

Having a good feel for where you are on the field can help you determine how hard or soft you have to shoot. If you are familiar with all the angles that a soccer game presents, you will know which part of the goal gives you the best option to shoot for. Determining where the defenders are gives you information on how much time and space you have to shoot and, perhaps, which angles are cut off and which are open so your shot will not be blocked. Knowing where the goalkeeper is positioned will help you gauge the most available part of the goal or whether you must chip it over her. And knowing all these things will help you choose which part of the foot (or head) is the right surface for the job.

Now, do you have time to think about all these things on the field as you are preparing to shoot? Of course not. Only diligent practice and game experience can hone these instincts.

When you get in shooting range, you must raise your game to a higher level. Why? Because the defenders, panicked by your close proximity to their precious goal, will be moving faster and harder. The space will be tighter, the time to shoot will be shorter, and because after so much hard work you have finally found yourself in a position to score, your anxiety will likely be higher as well.

This is why the best finishers take what the game gives them and maximize those opportunities. Often it is not the easiest option that gives you the best chance to score, because if it was, the defense wouldn't be doing its job. So if you see an opening, you seize it.

Should I bend the ball? Flick it with my head? Slot it in the corner? Drive it? Chip it? Poke it with my toe? Suffice it to say that you must do anything you can to get the ball into the net. If that means heading it off your nose or bouncing it off your knee, remember, pretty or not, all goals count the same.

I'll steal a saying from baseball (and change it a bit for soccer) because it really applies to being a great finisher: Kick it where they ain't. They, of course, being the goalkeeper.

As I've said before in this book, so much of soccer is deception, and there are so many ways to score. If you can keep the goalkeeper off balance and guessing (wrong, we hope) where you will shoot, you can sneak the ball into the net much more easily.

But let's go back to the most basic way of scoring: kicking the ball as hard as you can. There are few mo-

I got a bit under this one. Always try to put your shots on frame.

ments as exciting in soccer as a blistering shot from outside the penalty box that bulges the net. But keep in mind, the harder you hit the ball, the less control you have. When you take a bigger windup, which you need to get maximum power, you have to hit the ball perfectly to get it to go where you want. The good thing is that, like shooting from all distances and angles, you can practice this through much repetition. If you can combine power and accuracy, you can become deadly in front of the net, and that's the goal of all true finishers.

Shooting with power from long range—for our purposes we'll call that from 18 yards and farther—is a valuable tool. However, as much as I emphasize the importance of shooting when you get the chance, keep in mind that shooting when you are out of range probably will not help your team.

I see so many men players take shots from what seem like ridiculous distances. I figure that sometime in their career they scored a goal from that far out, so they always think they can do it again. This can be a healthy attitude, but we must be smart about what shots increase our percentage to score and when it might be wiser to attempt a pass to a teammate who might be in a better position to shoot.

As you grow stronger as a player, the distance from which you can score will be greater. If you feel like you're within this distance and have a good shot at putting the ball on the frame, pull the trigger. From long range, for most of us, this will be a shot hit with the instep and driven. When I shoot from long range, unless I have time to pick my head up and take a good look at the goal—which is rare, as I'm usually under a lot of pressure—I just think about getting it on the goal face.

I'll say it again: In shooting, technique is everything. If you really want to hit a ball hard, the first thing you have to do is be relaxed. That's one of the crazy ironies of shooting; sometimes your hardest shot is when you are most relaxed. This is where the technique comes in. If you swing with good technique, that ball can really fly. When you're tense and try to kill the ball, most likely you will overkick and send it everywhere except where you want it to go. For another example of this, look to golf. I've certainly power shanked a few tee shots in my time.

I think the best goal scorer ever to play our game is Michelle Akers. Not only does she have a shot that is probably measurably harder than anyone else's in the world (I

The Cannon. No one shoots with the power of Michelle Akers, and she can shoot as hard with her left foot as with her right. Here, she launches a rocket against Denmark in the Olympics.

swear I've heard the ball whistle through the air when she strikes a hard shot), but her sophistication in finishing is remarkable. Michelle scores goals through power and finesse and from all different angles. She scores them with her head, from close range, and from distances that other women don't dare to shoot from. I respect her so much, not only because of the amazing work she has put into becoming a finisher but because when that chance comes, Michelle buries it. That's the mark of a true finisher.

Michelle's shooting is legendary. The pure power behind her shots is something to behold. In our semifinal match against Denmark in the 1998 Goodwill Games, Michelle scored an unbelievable goal, ripping a spectacular, dipping, knuckling drive from 35 yards that flew into the left corner, giving the Danish goalkeeper no time to react. Rarely in men's or women's soccer does a shot go in from 35 yards without the goalkeeper even getting close to the ball. Michelle shoots to score, and she has better range than almost any player in the world. Her shots have such pace on them that they surprise goalkeepers, often forcing them to give up rebounds, which her teammates can exploit.

In our postgame interview session after that game, a reporter asked Michelle, "How surprised were you when the ball went in?" Michelle leaned forward to the microphone and answered in a matter-of-fact tone, "Not very." That is a perfect example of the mentality of great goal scorers: You have to possess confidence bordering on cockiness.

Perhaps the toughest thing about scoring is to believe the next chance will be the one where you put the ball in the net. As you advance through the higher levels of soccer, you will get fewer chances to score. A forward might only

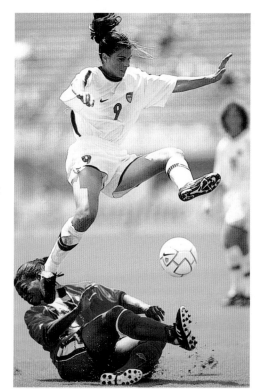

You have to understand that contact is part of the game.

isha draws first blood in our 1995 Women's World Cup opener against China.

◀ Whenever we play Norway, we give no quarter, nor do we expect any in return. But there's a difference between being physical and being violent, and a tackle from behind is officially the latter. The referee tosses the offending player.

Forwards shouldn't just hang around the midfield line calling for the ball. I take great pride in tracking back on defense whenever I can.

U-S-A! U-S-A! U-S-A!

Battling for the ball with Sweden's goalkeeper in the first game of the 1996 Olympics, I sprained my ankle so badly that Tisha and our trainer Patty Marchak had to carry me off the field. Luckily, I made it back for the semifinal and gold medal games.

We love our fans. Keep painting those faces and yelling yourselves hoarse!

I try to sign as many autographs as I can after a game,
but I can't sign them all. If I miss you, I'll catch you next time.

We won together: The 1999 Women's World Cup Champions.

Front row (l to r): Briana Scurry, Joy Fawcett, Kate Sobrero, me, Cindy Parlow, Julie Foudy, Carla Overbeck, Danielle Fotopolous, Brandi Chastain.

Second row (l to r): Assistant Coach Lauren Gregg, Head Coach Tony DiCicco, Shannon MacMillan, Sara Whalen, Christie Pearce, Tiffeny Milbrett, Tiffany Roberts, Kristine Lilly, Michelle Akers, Lorrie Fair.

Back row (l to r): Assistant Coach Jay Hoffman, Tracy Ducar, Tisha Venturini, Saskia Webber.

What can I say? Sometimes when I score I get carried away . . . literally!

get two really good chances in a game. I'm talking not about half chances but about quality chances, where everyone watching holds their breath for a second. Do you have the ability to put that ball away consistently? The players who do are the ones who become stars.

The mentality you must have as a scorer is an interesting dichotomy. You must have both a long memory and a short one. You must always learn from your mistakes, so you won't miss the same kind of shot again, but at the same time you must not dwell on your misses, not let them undermine your self-confidence. The thing about being a forward who is expected to score goals is that you will fail over and over again. You have to be very tough mentally and keep pounding away at a defense until it breaks. This takes maturity and a true understanding of what is best for the team.

In the Goodwill Games Gold Medal match against China, we were tied 0–0 after sixty-six minutes. China is a great team; you are not going to get very many chances to score against them, and when you do, they have an almost unbeatable goalkeeper. But in the sixty-sixth minute I got my chance when Kristine threaded a pass that unlocked the defense. I raced in one-on-one on the Chinese goalkeeper and drilled my shot into the left corner. I savor that goal because I got one chance near the end of the game and nailed it.

Three minutes from the end of the game I got another chance when a poor China clearance fell at my feet about 40 yards from the goal. I saw that the Chinese goalkeeper was caught too far from her line, so I took a touch and cracked a shot that flew over her and into the net to clinch the game.

Those goals were both examples of making the best of

A 40-yarder deserves more than a high five. Here I am sliding on my knees
in celebration after scoring the clincher against China in the finals of
the 1998 Goodwill Games.

what you're offered and using the correct shot to score in
each situation. The first was a driven instep shot, and the
second was a long chip. On those goals I definitely showed
how to be not just a shooter but a finisher.

But while the ability to fire a rocket from outside the
penalty box is certainly a weapon to be reckoned with,
most goals are scored within about 12 yards of the net. If
you are inside the penalty box, your finishing often has to
be of the one-touch variety because you just don't have a
lot of time and space. Many goals inside the penalty box
are created with a player going end line and pulling the ball
back in a seam for a teammate to finish first time. Here you

don't need a big windup but rather a short compact touch that redirects the ball with the inside of your foot. The premium is on accuracy and, once again, getting the ball on frame. But the ultimate is to finish every shot with your instep, maximizing your power and, with accuracy, giving the goalkeeper little chance to make a save.

When you watch some of the best finishers in the world, it seems as if they freeze time, especially in the penalty box. Amid a whirlwind of activity, cleats flying and huge bodies falling around them, they remain remarkably composed. They are merciless in punishing the slightest mistake and getting the job done quickly and efficiently.

That predatory calmness comes not only from working on your finishing in practice but also from the personality of the player—some people handle intense situations better than others. To finish at the highest level, you must be able to gather yourself in the penalty box when the pressure is at its highest and perform with finesse at high speed.

Is this easy? Absolutely not. As a matter of fact, scoring goals might just be the toughest and most frustrating skill in soccer. But once again, if it was easy, it wouldn't be such a special thing to score a goal.

One important thing to remember is that getting in position to shoot is as important as finishing itself. The greatest goal scorers have a knack for finding the gap in the defense, however fleeting, so that when a shot presents itself, it seems easy. One of the best examples of this is Gary Lineker, the former England star striker. He was what in England they call a "sniffer," someone who sniffs out goals, figures out where he needs to be, and then pounces on an opportunity. Lineker scored almost all of his goals inside the 12-yard line.

If a ball was crossed, he would dart in front of defenders and knock it in. If there were loose balls in the box, somehow he was always right there to cash in. The ability to put yourself in the best position to score is a talent partly born out of experience, but the great ones seem to have an innate feeling for finding the most dangerous position.

You also get several chances a game to score when you are not running into space; I'm talking about free kicks. It's amazing how many goals are scored from set plays, and to have someone on your team who excels at dead-ball situations is a huge advantage.

MICHELLE SAYS: There *is* a difference between a finisher and a shooter. Someone who just drills the ball is, in my mind, using a shotgun approach. There's a lot of power, but who knows where it's going? Finishing, on the other hand, is like using a rifle with a scope. It is powerful but precise and able to find the smallest of targets. The players who score tons of goals are the ones who can not only shoot but finish with deadly accuracy.

So, how did I become a finisher? First of all, I spent many hours losing some bad habits and refining my shooting technique as well as changing my mentality. I spent hours shooting at nothing but the net and then more hours shooting at garbage cans inside the goal and then more hours shooting at cones. I did this until I could do it almost perfectly without pressure. Then I threw in a goalkeeper, and once I beat him often enough, I added a defender, then two defenders for

On the National Team we have several players who are free-kick specialists. Why? Because they practice free kicks almost every day. At the end of our training sessions, Tony usually gives us ten minutes of free time to break into small groups and focus on drills in the areas where we feel we need the most work. There is always a cluster lined up outside the box with players alternating free kicks.

Again, when taking free kicks, it's important to try not to overpower the ball. Many players also fall victim to trying to spin or curve the ball too much and end up losing power. The ultimate free kick is a combination of a bending and driven

maximum pressure and intensity. After all that, you can see why those mammoth Norwegians and lightning-fast Chinese were hardly intimidating in Women's World Cup play.

Aside from the daily workouts of reviewing and reviewing (and reviewing some more) the basic techniques and tactics of finishing from every angle inside the 30, the main challenge I faced was maintaining the mentality of a hungry, risk-taking, confident goal scorer. I forced myself to take on players until I no longer feared anyone. In short, I became so confident I felt the only way someone could stop me would be if I messed up. I also trained myself to look to goal every time I got the ball. I always had in mind a way to get past someone or find a slight opening in order to get off a quick shot at goal. Goal scorers are like that. They think they can score from anywhere— and the good ones usually can.

ball that has enough movement to get over the wall and enough power to beat the goalkeeper to the spot.

When I take a free kick, I'm thinking about hitting it with a nice smooth stroke. I pick a spot over the wall; I'm not actually looking at the goal. I know the first thing I have to do is get it over the wall. If I hit the spot I'm aiming for over the wall, if my technique is relaxed and if I don't rush my swing, I'll get it on the frame. If it goes in, awesome; if not, hopefully it will be too tough for the keeper to handle cleanly—maybe a knuckleball or a hard bending shot—and the resulting rebound will present an opportunity one of my teammates will finish.

From a dead ball, I'm trying to bend my shot over a wall and into the goal. This is a skill you must practice, practice, practice.

I can't say I use visualization very much in shooting. Usually the game is happening too fast for me to visualize anything, but on free kicks I do try to picture the ball going just over the wall and under the crossbar. In practice, this can help you to develop the proper technique and become a master at free kicks.

From hitting dead balls we move to shooting on the run. Many times in a game you will be forced to shoot while dribbling on the run. This is difficult not only because the ball is moving but because there is a great possibility that you could be off balance, which can lead to inaccurate shots.

The key to shooting on the run is the preparation touch. When you are dribbling, you want to keep the ball close enough to you so that no one can poke it away, but as you prepare to shoot, you'll need a bit more space so that you can run onto the ball. You must develop this feel so that you can get into a good shooting rhythm.

Of course, power is important in shooting, and if you're strong, you can hit a better shot even if the ball is close to your body and you don't have much room to swing. But ideally, you will be able to take a full stride into the ball to send it on frame with velocity and accuracy. It's always good to sneak a peak at the goal as well, because the position of players in games is constantly changing and you need the most up-to-the-second information before unleashing your shot.

While you're dribbling, maybe the goalkeeper fell down; or perhaps she's giving you too much of one corner or has stepped out too far from her goal line and you can chip her. If you don't take a look up, you can hit a cracker of a shot and it will be saved, because what you really needed was just a nice bending ball on the ground into the corner.

One of the most difficult parts of shooting is volleying balls out of the air. It's something that girls don't seem to practice often enough. To be successful at it, you always have to keep your feet moving while the ball is in the air. Many times we see the ball coming and we grow roots. While it's in the air, sight it, judge where it will come down, and get to that spot at the same time the ball does or a bit earlier. The trick is to keep moving your feet, making many small adjustments instead of one large one. If you don't move to meet the ball, you will have to lunge forward or move backward at the last moment and shoot off balance, and that is not a recipe for success.

Most people don't realize it, but they usually sight the ball in the air and watch it coming in, then when it is about head-high and dropping to their foot they take their eye off the ball. *Whiff!* Timing is key, and split-second timing, of course, comes from practice, but everyone can start by watching the ball all the way to her foot.

One mistake players make is believing that a shot means only one chance to score. This couldn't be farther from the truth. Every shot has a potential rebound, off the goalkeeper or off the frame itself, and you must be ready to capitalize on that.

Being a finisher on rebounds is a matter of disciplining yourself to react more quickly than the defender, to crash the goal every time a shot is taken. Many times when your teammate shoots, players react by relaxing as if the attack is over. The great finishers never stop until the ball is in the goalkeeper's arms, out of bounds, or in the net. When someone shoots, you have to condition yourself to follow the ball, even if you are the one taking the shot. As we've said, if the ball is hit on frame, anything can happen. If the goalkeeper mishandles the ball and no one is following up, it's a wasted opportunity.

Kristine Lilly is one of the best on the National Team at what we call "framing" the goal. Against Argentina in April

Sight the ball.

Connect with
the laces.

Follow
through!

of 1998, she was right there in front of the goal when a rebound bounced off the goalkeeper. But Kristine overran the ball a bit and could only hit it on the bounce behind her with the back of her heel. Miraculously, it popped over her head like a rainbow and into the goal. Usually finishing rebounds is a matter of slamming the ball into the net from close range, but Kristine takes it to another level.

Finally, we can't forget acrobatics in shooting. By this I mean diving headers, bicycle kicks, and flying side volleys. It is valuable to master these fancy shots because it gives you more opportunities to score goals, but by no means do I recommend that you practice bicycle kicks—that can be dangerous.

Still, it is important to remember that you must be willing to take the physical risk to get the ball into the net, and that sometimes means hurtling yourself through the air for a diving header or reaching high and falling to volley a cross. Sometimes that's the only way to get the ball past the goalkeeper, and you have to have the courage to sacrifice your body for the team.

If you want to practice these shots, start slowly. Watch the professional players execute the fantastic finishes, mess around with your friends by volleying crosses and maybe trying some falling headers, and one day you might amaze yourself in a game.

Technique

When shooting a ball with your instep, once again, it is vitally important that you point your toe straight down and keep your ankle locked. This will help you get the most

Many times you have to give up your body to score. Here, Kristine Lilly does just that against Norway.

power and give you the most surface on the laces of your shoes with which to hit the ball. As you try to keep the ball low and on frame, it is also key that your plant foot is even with the ball and that the knee of your kicking foot is over the ball. Getting your knee over the ball will help you lean forward and take advantage of the power that comes from your hip swinging your leg through the ball. If your plant foot is too far behind the ball, you'll be reaching for the ball as you kick and your body will lean back, causing your foot to get under the ball and your shot to go high.

If you're going to bend the ball as you shoot, the key is not so much to kick it using the inside or outside of your foot but rather to strike it slightly off center, generating spin. But for the ball to truly bend and curve, it must be well struck and hit just a bit on the side of your laces to the inside or outside of your shoe.

To get maximum power out of your shots, you must follow straight through the ball. Often you'll see players follow through so well that they end up with their shooting foot hitting the ground first as they kick through the ball—the force of their own kick turning them in the air.

A good volley is executed not with a full leg swing but with a short snap of the lower leg. You must make sure your hip gets above the ball so you can keep the ball down. And don't be afraid to leave your feet and hit a falling volley! Sometimes that's the only way you can get that hip above the ball and follow through. Besides, it look pretty spectacular when you connect.

As Michelle said earlier, repetition of shooting technique under numerous different conditions will help you find your rhythm and comfort area, so that when you get that rare chance in a game, you will be the finisher that every team needs.

Shooting Games/Drills

Keys to remember:
- Keep your toe down.
- Keep your ankle locked.
- Follow through to target.
- Strike solidly with your chosen surface: laces, outside or inside of the foot.
- Relax; don't try to kick too hard.
- Shoot on the frame.

You and a Bag of Balls

Obviously, the best way to improve your shooting is just to shoot. Not so much that you pull your quadriceps muscle, but enough that you get in a good workout, practicing different types of shots from different angles into both corners of the goal, high and low. You should practice shooting on the run, hitting dead balls, and connecting off crosses (if you have someone to serve balls). You can turn a bag of balls, a goal, and your little sister or brother to chase errant shots into a great workout. (Don't forget to let the kid take some shots too!) Try to take ten shots from each distance and angles, and challenge yourself to increase the number of quality shots each training session.

Four-Corner Shooting

This drill is done with your team, with two goals positioned about 25 to 30 yards apart. Gather the soccer balls at the same post on each goal. Divide the team in half, with a

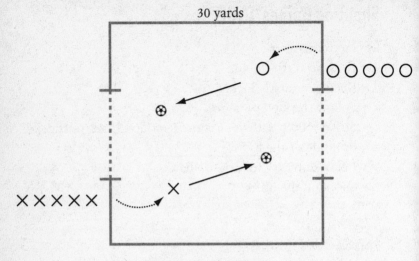

30 yards

FOUR-CORNER SHOOTING

group lined up by each goal. Take one or two touches and strike your shot, then change lines. You can get many shots in a short period of time. Concentrate on hitting a solid shot on the frame. Don't kill it! The power will come with practice and good technique.

Power/Finesse

A group of players starts 30 yards from the goal with the soccer balls at one post. One player at the post serves a pass on the ground that you hit with power from about 20 yards away. You continue your run as you follow your shot, and a second pass is played in a rhythm where you strike it about 14 yards from the goal. This second shot you try to place, or finesse, into one of the corners. This is not an easy drill for goalkeepers who are facing shot after shot in quick succession, but it's great for shooting on the run and to practice both power and placement.

Four versus Four in the Penalty Box

There are few drills more fun than Four versus Four on big goals. Shooting is the name of the game here, and as you should most likely play in a 30 × 44-yard grid (30 yards long with the width of the penalty box), every time you get the ball you are in range. The emphasis is on taking as many shots as possible while your team is on the field, but remember, if there is someone in a better position to shoot, pass it to her. Otherwise, pull the trigger again and again. Usually, you play three- or four-minute games with the winner staying on.

TEN

Heading

Soccer's Own Skill

Heading is a skill unique to soccer. In any other sport, if you hit the ball with your head (or if the ball hits you), something bad has happened. Soccer players should take pride in their ability to head the ball. In what other sport do athletes "use their head" so literally?

Some of soccer's most spectacular plays come off headers, and your team's ability to win balls in the air, both offensively and defensively, can play a major role in deciding a match. It's a simple fact that the game is played both in the air and on the ground, and to excel at soccer, you must be adept at controlling the ball whether it is above your head or at your feet.

The importance of being a proficient header on both offense and defense cannot be overstated. Michelle Akers headed in the first goal in the 1991 Women's World Cup final, and in that same game Norway answered with its own goal off a header. Fortunately, Michelle scored another goal with her feet to win the game and give us the championship.

Just as critical as ruling the air in the opponent's penalty box is your ability to win head balls in front of your own goal. So many times a head ball won by the defense starts the attack. From defense, goes the saying, comes offense. Playing against Denmark in the 1996 Olympics, Michelle Akers won a ball in midfield and sent such a powerful header back toward the Danish defense that I was able to run onto it for a breakaway and score our second goal of the game. This is just one example, but it clearly illustrates how important it is to win balls in the air, not only to prevent the opponent from scoring but to create scoring opportunities for your team.

You've probably heard it said that soccer games are won in the midfield. Another way to put it is: Midfielders must dominate the air. Consistently winning tackles on the ground and balls in the air keeps the pressure on the other team's defense; eventually they will crack.

Our defenders on the U.S. team—Carla Overbeck, Joy Fawcett, Brandi Chastain, Kate Sobrero, Christie Pearce, and Lorrie Fair—are overpowering in the air. If you are not a good header, you'll have a harder time trying to make it to the highest levels of soccer. Every soccer player has experienced some pain while heading a ball, but if it is done with the correct technique and mind-set, heading is not only painless but can be one of the most fun things to do on a soccer field.

Concentration is key. If you have confidence in your ability to hit the ball on the right part of your forehead and drive it in the direction you want it to go, you will attack every header. But how do you gain that confidence? No surprise here: repetition. Repetition develops muscle memory

Brandi skies above three Icelanders in the penalty box.

I've always said Michelle Akers is head and shoulders above the rest.

for the proper technique and is the key to mastering any soccer skill.

Every time you head a ball, you want to make contact with what I call the "sweet spot"—the flat part of your forehead that is a little smaller than your palm, just below your hairline. While the sweet spot can vary an inch or maybe two, if you head the ball too far on the top of your head, not only will it hurt, but most of the time the ball will go astray. Of course, if you head it too low, your nose will get an up-close introduction to the soccer ball, and no one wants that.

Another important factor to remember is that you must always play the ball, not let it play you. Many times young players let the ball hit them in the head instead of attacking the ball. If you want to be an effective header, you can't be passive. Being aggressive allows you to dictate where the ball goes.

Basically, there are two types of heading: offensive and defensive. They are done with almost the same technique but with entirely different goals in mind. We'll start with defensive heading because, as I've said, you've got to win the ball before you can attack and score.

When heading on defense, you always want to try to direct the ball to one of your teammates so you can retain possession. However, your first priority is to get the ball away from your goal, especially if you are deep in your defensive third. You want to head the ball up and out—high in the air to give your defense a chance to regroup, and out to put distance between the ball and your goal. On the National Team, our defenders do a functional training drill in which long balls are chipped into them and they compete by seeing who can head the ball the farthest down the field.

To head the ball for distance in the air, you want to hit it on its lower half to give it some loft. Heading balls down into the other team's onrushing forwards is a great way to get scored on, and it happens quite often. Distance and loft are important, but so is direction. Head the ball toward the sidelines, never straight back into the middle of the field. If you can master both distance and direction, you can be assured that the ball will be out of danger, at least temporarily.

By contrast, in offensive heading, you want to head the ball down. I've never heard anyone say that you headed the ball too low when heading on goal, but how many headers have you seen fly over the crossbar? Heading the ball down so it bounces on the goal line before going into the net makes it very tough for the goalkeeper to save.

Of course, you want to have your head above the ball so you can make contact on the ball's upper half and drive it down and into the goal. Often, if you really concentrate on hitting the ball just above the midline, even if you mishit it, it still has a chance of going into the goal. I've never heard a striker complain about a sore nose when the ball went in the net!

Head goals are often scored when the attacker redirects the ball with her head, using the force of the cross (which is often substantial) to glance it into the net. In game situations timing is vitally important. You can have great technique, but if your timing is off, you're much less likely to succeed. Most of the time while heading in a game you'll be jumping. If you can time your leap so you leave the ground a split second before your opponent and strike the ball at the top of your jump, you'll have a much better chance of winning the duel.

Tisha Venturini is one of the best headers in the world. Her timing and body control are remarkable as she seemingly hangs in the air for a full second before meeting the ball. You rarely see her jump too early or too late. Michelle Akers, also fantastic in the air, takes full advantage of her 5-foot-10 frame to dominate aerial battles in the midfield. Tisha is 5 feet 6 inches tall, yet she wins almost every contested head ball. Like the great Pelé, who was only 5 feet 8 inches, she has scored many goals off headers through timing, speed, and an uncanny sense for getting to the ball.

Both Tisha and Michelle also possess another key element in being a successful header, and that's bravery. Neither shies away from the tangle of flying arms and legs, the undercutting defenders, the desperate melee that erupts whenever the ball is crossed into the penalty box. A ball off the nose or an elbow in the face is an occupational hazard for goal scorers. It's only natural to be afraid of something flying at your head, but the great ones learn not to flinch.

When I was eleven, I jumped up behind a girl and tried to head a ball but instead connected with the back of her head. Ouch! I mashed my nose and bled all over the place. After that, I was understandably a little nervous about challenging opponents in the air. But I got over my fear in practice by constantly forcing myself to jump and head balls in crowds, until I was so sick of the heading drills I forgot to be afraid. I also came to understand that if I went into head challenges tentatively, I would probably get smacked in the face, but if I went in aggressively, I was more likely to win the ball.

Proper technique and mind-set will help you avoid the hard knocks and make heading pain-free and fun. Remember, your forehead is one of the toughest spots on your body, mostly because nature has determined that it's the area that needs the most protection.

A major component of good heading technique is using your arms, not only to help you jump and for balance but also to create a pocket of space between you and the opponent; this will give you room to win the ball. Almost all headers, like most jump shots in basketball, are contested. You are always jockeying for position on defensive headers and many times on the offensive end as well. While you don't want to push the opponent outright—referees love to whistle a good shove in the back—bumping, tugging, and jostling, within reason, are an accepted part of the game.

Compete for every header, because even if you're unlikely to win the ball—say you're out of position or the other girl is much taller than you—you might knock the opponent off balance, insuring that she doesn't get a clean shot at the ball. Don't foul, though! Go straight up and go up strong. Too many players push in the back if they're going to lose a head ball. Getting side-on position instead of directly behind a player will help. This way, you won't have to come from behind or try to jump over her to get to the ball.

Soccer is a physical game, and heading is a big part of that. You must be equipped to survive those head battles. And as with all skills, it's best to start young.

As Tisha points out, you must master the art of connecting with the ball at the top of your leap, while fighting off airborne opponents. If you can at least get a piece of the ball, even if it doesn't go exactly where you want, your teammates may win that second ball on the ground.

I have never thought I was very good at heading, and it's something that I really concentrate on in practice. Still, I have scored more than a few goals with my head, and part of that comes from being in good position.

I'm not the type of player, like Michelle or Tisha, who will power the ball past anyone from 15 yards out. I score head goals by timing my jumps and runs in the penalty box and by slipping in front of defenders to nod the ball in. I have played with some of my teammates for so long that I can anticipate their crosses, dart in to meet a cross with my head, and put it on frame.

Many people may remember my one hundredth career

international goal against Russia in Rochester, New York, at the Nike U.S. Women's Cup '98. It was a driven shot with my instep that flew under the crossbar. But I was just as proud of my hundred and first goal in that game, which was from a header. Tiffeny Milbrett crossed a ball from the right corner of the penalty box, and I sliced through the middle and flew through the air (well, truth be told, I actually kind of fell) to redirect the ball into the left corner.

I didn't jump over anyone. The goal was a product of good technique, precise timing, and, of course, a great pass from Tiffeny.

One other aspect of heading that we should touch upon is how to handle those 50- to 60-yard goalkeeper punts and goal kicks, which can be incredibly difficult to head. This is true whether you are a forward trying to keep the ball in your attacking half of the field or a defender trying to keep it out of your defensive third. The keys that we have talked about in this chapter once again come into play here.

First you must "sight" the ball. This is similar to an outfielder in baseball determining where a fly ball is going to land so he knows

Low-bridged!
Now that's taking things too far!

whether he needs to move forward, backward, or sideways. This is not an easy task, and the ability to sight long balls comes from watching countless spinning balls fly at you from different heights and angles over a long period of time.

Of course, the ideal is not to go right to the point where the ball will land but to give yourself a couple of steps to run at the ball so you can launch yourself into the air. This isn't always possible when an opponent is contesting the ball. That's where the jockeying comes in. Some defenders I have squared up against are just so darn tall that the best I can do is simply get in their way. If a Norwegian player is 7 inches taller than me (and I've played against players that big), then I'm not going to win many headers, but it doesn't mean I'm not going to jump for every ball.

I'll say it again: Contest every ball in the midfield. As a forward, I love it when defenders let a ball drop, giving me a much better shot at winning a bouncing ball. Even if you head the ball straight up or out of bounds, it delays the counterattack and gives your teammates time to properly position the defense.

A few words on diving headers: I know it's tough to remember when you're flying parallel to the ground and worried about breaking your fall or crashing into a defender, but you must never forget to keep your head up. Many young players hit the ball off the top of their head instead of on their forehead. Whether you're stock-still or doing you best impersonation of Superwoman, the technique is the same. Yes, you may get skinned knees and elbows, but it's worth it if you score a spectacular goal.

TISHA SAYS: My older brother Todd and I used to have heading competitions in our house. We would jump up and try to head at a spot on the wall. Sounds kind of strange, I know, but it was really competitive, and I always wanted to jump higher and be better than him. As a matter of fact, I used to beat him all the time.

I played a lot of soccer with boys when I was growing up in Modesto, California. If you haven't heard of Modesto, I won't hold it against you, but there just weren't a lot of girls playing soccer there. By playing with boys, I was forced to learn how to head when I was around ten because they were so much more aggressive. We practiced heading so much that it became one of my favorite things. I remember doing diving headers in mud. When you're ten, diving headers in mud are awesome. Now I only dive in the mud if have really have to.

By playing soccer with boys, I learned good technique by watching them and competing against them. It really forced me to learn how to time my jumps well, because a lot of the time the boys were taller. I have no doubt that it really helped me in my game today because everyone thinks that I have such a great vertical jump, but really I don't—it's mostly timing.

When Mom made us take our soccer outside, I would spend hours in our backyard with my brother. He used to cross off the back lawn to the driveway, and the open garage door was the goal. We had to make sure there were no cars in there, or Mom would get mad, but I scored a lot of head goals into that garage.

Mia talks about being brave on your headers, and I think that is one of the most important lessons for young girls to learn. You have to go up without fear. You must always attack the ball. When heading on goal, you have more finesse than in defensive heading. You have to be more precise in your placement, and you really need to be active in the penalty box, so you can be in the right place at the right time to head in those crosses.

So while it's fun to score a goal, I get great satisfaction in fighting for position under an opponent's goal kick, meeting it at the top of my jump, and bashing it back into their defensive third. Not only is it fun, but as Mia says, it helps you win games because the pressure is always on the other team's defense.

Air Venturini.

Technique

For heading technique, the most important thing to remember is to keep your eyes open and your mouth closed. You must be able to watch the ball until the moment of contact. When you close your eyes, well, that's when you get hit on the nose. Keeping your mouth closed will prevent you from biting your tongue and will protect your teeth. I've chomped my tongue a few times, and I know I don't want to do it again.

Although you're hitting the ball with your head, most of

Arch your back and follow through. Remember to keep your eyes open and your mouth closed.

the power comes from using your whole body. You have to arch your back and whip your upper torso and neck to snap into the ball. You want to contact the ball as your body is jackknifing forward, not too early and not too late, or you will have less power and control. You use your body almost like a slingshot; the farther back you bend, the more power you will have as you move into the ball.

A leaping header can be even more powerful, as you incorporate your whole body into the snapping motion. Using the same technique as for your upper body and head,

Bend at the waist
and snap into the ball.

tuck your legs back as you jump, then kick them forward as you power through the ball. Timing is critical and this move requires plenty of practice, but the reward is watching a properly struck ball sail downfield.

Heading Games/Drills

Keys to remember:
- Keep your eyes open, mouth closed.
- Keep your hands out for balance and protection.
- Contact the ball on the "sweet spot" of your forehead.
- Bend at the waist, and snap your body into the ball.
- Follow through to target.
- Attack the ball!

Heading Progression

This drill should be done with a partner. Because heading can at first seem like an odd skill to learn, it's best for young players to start the process sitting down. Sit on your backside in the sit-up position (legs forward, knees up and bent), and have your partner throw the ball to you so you can head it as you snap forward. The service is key to a productive drill, so make sure your partner tosses the ball with both hands. It may take a couple of throws for her to get the hang of sending the ball where you want it. You can then move onto your knees, snapping forward as you head the ball and catching yourself as you fall on your hands.

Now you are ready to head from your feet. Practice both heading the ball back to your partner standing square to her and also with one foot forward. Then progress to jumping to head the ball, off one foot and then both, as your partner varies the throws so that you have to concentrate to meet them in the air. If you want to ease into this drill and perfect your technique, have your partner hold the ball up so you can jump and head a stationary target. Obviously, this won't work if your partner is much shorter than you. Finally, you can head while moving forward and having your partner serve while you're moving backward. You can do this drill while jumping to head the ball or just running through it to bullet a header back into your partner's hands.

Chip and Head to Score or Clear

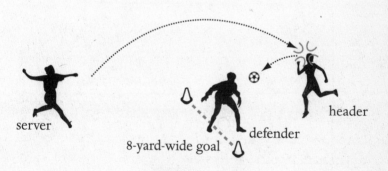

server

8-yard-wide goal

defender

header

CHIP AND HEAD TO SCORE

This drill requires three players. Two are positioned about 30 yards apart on either side of an 8-yard-wide goal, which is guarded by the third player. One player serves a ball in the air over the goal to the other player, who attempts to head it by the goalkeeper. Switch headers, servers, and goalkeepers. The player who scores the most headers out of ten serves wins.

You can also work on defensive heading in this drill. Instead of heading the ball on goal, the player tries to clear it over an imaginary crossbar, as if defending a dangerous cross close to the goal mouth. Sometimes it's better to give up a corner kick than to try a clearance from your own goal line. Height and distance count in this variation, and any header that can be touched by the goalkeeper doesn't count for points. All you servers, remember to make your teammates look good.

Two versus Two Heading

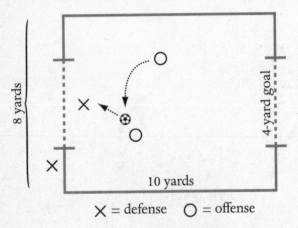

X = defense   O = offense

TWO VERSUS TWO HEADING

This is a fun drill using four players in an 8 × 10-yard grid with two goals about 6 to 8 yards wide. One of the defenders plays in goal while the other stands behind the goal and is not involved in the play. You start with a service from your hands. The offensive partners must keep the ball in the air with their heads until they are close enough to shoot (but only with a header) on the goalkeeper, who can use her hands. If the ball drops to the ground, if it hits anything but an offensive player's head, or if the opposing goalkeeper makes a save, possession goes to the other team. You can pull off some cool diving headers in this game, but be careful not to slam into the goalkeeper/defender!

ELEVEN

Goalkeeping

The Last Line of Defense

I know a few things about goalkeepers. First of all, I love to score on them. But what soccer player doesn't? Second, it's the most important position on the field and one of the most difficult. Third, there have been four players in the history of the U.S. Women's National Team who have played goalkeeper in a World Cup game. Mary Harvey played all the games at the 1991 Women's World Cup in China. At the 1995 Women's World Cup in Sweden, we had three players who played in goal: our starter, Briana Scurry; her backup, Saskia Webber—and me.

Yes, it's a little-known fact that I pulled on the gloves in Sweden. Until that time, my goalkeeping experience had

A rare photograph of me in Briana Scurry's goalkeeper uniform at the 1995 Women's World Cup in Sweden. Take a good look—you'll never see me in that jersey again!

been limited to some end-of-practice crossing drills where my teammates took great delight in nailing me with the ball, but I guess I saved a few, because somehow the coaches decided that it was I who should step between the pipes.

It went like this.

We were playing our second Women's World Cup match of the first round at Stromvallen Stadium in a little town called Gavle. We were ahead of Denmark, 2–0, in the waning moments of the game, when the unbelievable happened. Briana picked up a ball in the penalty box with no pressure on her and went to punt it up the field. It was a seemingly innocuous play, one we've seen a thousand times before. Well, apparently as she went to punt, she barely stepped over the edge of the penalty box before releasing the ball. The linesman raised his flag, waved it around like they do, and the referee came running over. Usually the referee would just call a hand ball and give Denmark a free kick at the top of the penalty box. This referee, however, decided to interpret the rules a little too literally and gave Briana a red card for intentionally handling the ball even though there was no one near her!

We were all in a state of shock for a few minutes, and then our assistant coach, April Heinrichs, called me over to the sideline. April was the captain of the 1991 Women's World Cup championship team. She put her arm around me and said very calmly, because I'm sure she didn't want to freak me out, "Mia, we've used all our substitutes, and we're going to put you in goal. How do you feel about that?"

It didn't really register fully, and I replied, "Why don't you use a real goalkeeper?" After all, we had two on the bench.

"We've used all our subs," she repeated. And then it dawned on me: We had already used three field players as substitutes! The rules only allow for three, and I was about to get some on-the-job training in the nets.

The first thought that entered my mind then was that Denmark still had a free kick from 19 yards out and they had a huge sweeper who could really crush the ball. Her name was Kamma Flaeng, and Kamma didn't fool around.

Yes, my international goalkeeping debut was to face a free kick about as close to the goal as could be without it being a penalty shot from a woman who would like nothing better than to blast me halfway across the Atlantic.

I really don't remember what I was thinking at the time, but looking back, I realize I wasn't well positioned. I was too far behind the wall instead of shaded toward the open part of the net (that's goalkeeper talk, thank you). Well, wouldn't you know it? Kamma took a big run up and sent the ball sailing over the crossbar. I like to think I would have saved it anyway, but of course, we'll never know!

I ended up touching the ball just twice. I didn't have to make any flying saves. I collected a ball that came bouncing through the defense and punted it as far

A good goalkeeper can save your team over and over again. Bri has nerves of steel.

from goal as I could. For my last touch in goal, I smothered a low-liner off a crossed ball for my one credited save in Women's World Cup play.

Our sweeper, Carla Overbeck, came up to me after the game, and I think her words probably summed up the feeling of the whole team: "You know, Mia, I was pretty confident with you going back there—I mean, you're a good athlete—until I turned around and you looked about the size of a peanut in the goal." I think it was probably then that the defense made a silent pact to not let anyone shoot on me. I'm happy to say they did their job and we escaped with a shutout and the victory.

But even before my brief fling in the different-colored

BRIANA SAYS: Courage in goalkeeping is so important. Many aspects of the position require that you stick your head into places most people wouldn't dare. Sometimes you get kicked in places any sane person definitely wouldn't want to get kicked in, but that's just part of the job.

You have to play every game with confidence, and that confidence has to be real, and it has to be evident to those playing with you and against you. You must have an aura about you that says, "Things are under control in *my* penalty box." All your catches must be solid, you must never be indecisive, and you must always rule the air! All good goalkeepers have this presence in the nets.

But no doubt, to be a good keeper, you must be willing to work at it and work hard. Goalkeeper training is physically demanding and very fatiguing. You are constantly hitting the ground, getting back up, and diving again. You must be one of the fittest players on the team. Your training is a bit different from that of the other players, as it is more anaerobic than aerobic, but goalkeepers should take pride in working harder than jersey, I had tremendous respect for goalkeepers and what they do. Goalkeepers are defined by how well they handle pressure. Depending on the game, they may not see much action, but then all of a sudden the ball comes flying at them, and their reaction can determine the outcome of the game. If they can make one big save, perhaps their teammates will remember. But if they allow a goal, no one will ever forget.

everyone else. You must still try to be a good long-distance runner like your field-player teammates. Goalkeeping can also be painful, especially when you have Mia Hamm and Michelle Akers shooting at you mercilessly from 12 yards away.

If you get scored on—and every goalkeeper does—you must have the mentality to bounce back right away. Some goalkeepers lose their composure after they let a goal in, but the great ones shake it off because that next save might be the one that wins the game for your team. If you dwell on your mistakes, another ball will be whizzing past your ear before you know it.

Finally, as a goalkeeper, you must take pride in your responsibility to the team as the last defender. Your team must know that they can depend on you. Even on the National Team there are defensive breakdowns, and when the shots do come, your teammates need to know that you will be there to bail them out.

That kind of respect is not given. You have to earn it. The harder you fight for the team, the more ferociously they will battle for you.

A goalkeeper's concentration has to be nigh unbreakable. I'd go as far as saying that it has to be almost perfect for ninety minutes in order to excel at the position. If I make a mistake on the forward line because of lack of focus, it won't necessarily cost us the game, but if a goalkeeper relaxes in back, it might.

You can have a great team, but if your goalkeeper is weak, it will almost always come back to haunt you. Luckily, we have one of the best in the world in Briana Scurry. In big games Bri is so calm, it radiates throughout the entire team. In addition to her mental toughness, she is a phenomenal athlete—cat-quick, powerful, and brave.

Goalkeepers also have to be as good with their eyes and mouth as they are with their hands and feet. Because the goalkeeper is the only player capable of seeing the whole field, a vocal keeper can help organize your defense by alerting you to unmarked defenders or to plays developing behind you. But don't just yell to yell! Your talk must be productive, or you can become a detriment.

These days, your goalkeeper also has to be very good at playing the ball with her feet. With teams increasingly lining up without a true sweeper and with a flat-back four, the goalkeeper must now become a sweeper-keeper. You must have confidence that if you pass the ball to your goalkeeper, she can either trap it, make a smart pass, or drive it 50 yards up the field. This gives defenders an important escape hatch when pressured.

Always remember that not only is the goalkeeper the last defender, she is also the first player on offense and often starts the attack. It is important that her distribution with her hands and feet—her passes, throws, and punts—be high-quality so her teammates have good options after they receive the ball.

The National Team goalkeepers work on their distance kicking almost every day in training. I know that very few youth goalkeepers take time to practice goal kicks and punts. But working for ten minutes per day on long balls will pay dividends down the line.

It's tough to get a ball past the cat-quick Briana Scurry.

On young teams, it's not a bad idea to have everyone take a turn in goal so that they can appreciate the awesome responsibility of the position. Maybe you will even become the next Briana Scurry. After all, she started as a forward.

Through the years, I've developed a deep admiration for goalkeepers. They have the power to turn agony into ecstasy in a single moment. We all know the feeling we get when an opponent has a point-blank scoring chance that's sure to go in. Your stomach drops, your heart skips a beat and you can't breathe. Then your goalkeeper comes up with an spectacular diving save and the rush of adrenaline (relief!) makes you want to run over and hug her.

Not only has she given your team a boost, but she has also forced the other team to go back to work to earn another scoring chance, which never comes easily. This is when good teams take advantage of an opponent's letdown after a narrowly missed opportunity to score a quick counterattacking goal.

That's why goalkeepers are as important to offense as they are to defense. They are the last players to stop an attack and the first to start a counterattack. They deserve tremendous credit not only for the responsibilities they carry on their backs, but for the physical and emotional risk they subject themselves to every day.

Constantly ask yourself, "Have you hugged your goalkeeper today?"

PART III

The Complete Player

TWELVE

Consistency

Michael Jordan . . . Cal Ripken . . . John Elway . . . Pelé . . . Kristine Lilly . . . Besides being extraordinary athletes in their respective sports, what is it that truly sets them apart? Did they all rise from relative obscurity to become superstars? Did they all lead their teams to a world championship? Are they all fans of Adam Sandler movies?

Well, the first two are certainly true, and I know for a fact that Kristine has seen *Happy Gilmore* seventeen times. But the distinguishing characteristic that they all have in common is their ability to maintain a remarkably high level of play from game to game, season to season, and championship to championship—they embody consistency.

Consistency is the hallmark of greatness. When people start talking about who's the world's greatest soccer player,

I say Kristine Lilly is the best player in the world.

I tend to sidestep the accolade and look to Kristine Lilly, who I truly believe deserves the tag more than anyone else.

I have never been one to keep track of statistics, and I guess I lost count of just how many games Kristine has played, because I was astounded when I happened to see the numbers that she has put up in her career. She was the first woman to play one hundred times for the USA, and during her entire career she has only come off the bench four times! She has started every other game she has played and will no doubt be the first player in history to play two hundred times for her country, a plateau thought impossible to reach before Kristine redefined consistency in soccer. She has missed only eight National Team games since she debuted as a sixteen-year-old in 1987 and has played in nearly 90 percent of the matches that the team has played in its history! And honestly, I can't recall a single bad game. But if you'd ask her, I'm sure she would say she rarely plays to her potential. It's this attitude of never being satisfied with her performance, along with her incredible versatility, that makes me and anyone who has ever had to mark her shake their head in disbelief. Kristine is awesome. I know I might be a hero to many young girls out there, but Kristine is my hero.

Whether she's tearing down the flanks to deliver a perfectly weighted cross, slashing into the box to nail a half volley, or somehow sprinting 75 yards back on defense to strip an opponent of the ball, she is a factor in *every* game.

Playing with Kristine for twelve years, first at North Carolina and then on the National Team, has made me strive harder for consistency. I look at her fitness and nutritional regimen and I'm inspired to push myself that extra lap. Most mistakes are made late in the game when your tank is almost empty, but Kristine is running as hard in the eighty-first minute as she was in the eleventh. Her mental and physical stamina make her the most dependable player on the team.

When I analyze my game and how I've progressed through the years, I see a player who no longer relies on pure athleticism to beat opponents and score goals. If the direct approach isn't working, I have options. If the dribble isn't there, I look for the pass. If my passing is off, I ratchet up my defense. Work to be a well-rounded player, so if one element of your game breaks down, another will compensate. Versatility is at the heart of consistency.

When I first started with the National Team I was understandably timid, and some of the decisions I made on the field were just plain poor. I recall many unnecessarily rushed passes, countless unproductive runs, and lots of butchered scoring chances. Because I studied these missed opportunities, I make better decisions today and have achieved a level of consistency I'm proud of, even if it's not in Kristine's league.

Any player on the National Team will tell you that approaching every game with the same level of mental intensity is the hardest part of being consistent. Every match must be treated with equal importance, no matter if you are playing the worst team in the league or the best team in the world. The surest way to get upset is to underestimate your opponent. This focus on your own game and not on how good or bad an opponent may be will help you be mentally prepared for every match. But to be a championship team, all eleven players must perform at this high level over the course of the entire season.

We won the Women's World Cup in 1991, lost in the semifinals in 1995, and then won the Olympics in 1996. Some people may consider two world titles consistency, but we don't share that view. Two out of three doesn't cut it for us. We want to be part of a dynasty, the kind of team that is remembered for winning every championship they ever played in.

Another way to put it, with apologies to my teammates who didn't play there, is we want to be the North Carolina of world soccer. Since 1983 (when the NCAA began having a national women's soccer championship tournament), the University of North Carolina has come out on top thirteen of sixteen times. Without a doubt, the program has had a wealth of world-class talent over the years, but to win on such a consistent basis, you need more than talent.

One of the reasons is the approach to the game that Anson Dorrance instills in his players. It's a mixture of a powerful sense of team and family, which causes you to battle for one other, and individual responsibility to be the best you can be, which motivates you to fight for yourself. Anson established this attitude in the National Team—he coached the United States from 1986 to 1994—and this philosophy remains as strong as ever today, under Tony DiCicco.

At UNC we would generally play games on Friday and Sunday and then have Monday off. Tuesday was mainly a fitness day, with an emphasis on personal training. After all, fitness is just you against you. Wednesdays we played one-on-one and small-sided games, which put a premium on individual performance. Two days before a game we would

Tisha (back row, left of guy in baseball cap) and me (kneeling far left) with the legendary 1992 UNC championship team. It's great to be part of a dynasty.

play a full-field scrimmage, starters against the reserves, applying what we had worked on alone in the context of the team as a whole. The day before a game, Anson put us through a number of shooting and finishing drills that were as much about team bonding as they were about serious instruction. It was this progression from individual to team and back again that gave us an appreciation for how all the different parts can mesh together into one smooth-running machine.

Another ingredient in UNC's success is Anson's dedication to the idea that if you truly understand how something works, you will be better at it. He never took the basics for granted. Through Zen-like instruction, he made us real students of the game and did his best to eliminate any surprises. On the field our play was not just a robotic execution of what he had taught us but a fluid expression of the lessons learned.

The UNC dynasty was built on talent, dedication to team and individual excellence, and a ravenous curiosity about the nuances of the sport. I'd like to think that someday, even if I'm no longer playing, the U.S. Women's National Team will still have the same aura of invincibility and consistency.

THIRTEEN

Being a Winner

How many times have our parents trotted out the tired old line "Winning isn't everything," and how many times have you rolled your eyes and thought to yourself, "Yeah, sure"? The next day or the next game we might agree with our parents, but right after a loss, it sure seems like it's everything. If winning isn't everything, why is it that we fight so hard to achieve it and feel so empty and miserable when we don't? It's the feeling of knowing you were the best on that day and conversely, when you lose, it's the painful awareness that you just didn't get it done that sticks with you for so long.

I've got to admit that I'm addicted to winning and have

been fortunate enough to win a lot of games in my life. The truth is, early on, when my brother Garrett used to whip me in backyard games of one-on-one, I developed a keen distaste for losing and dedicated myself to not letting it happen too often. If you want to be a winner, it starts with this determination to strive for victory—fairly, squarely, decently, by the rules—but always to win.

Winning, of course, is as much about how you play the game as it is about who's ahead when the final whistle blows. I'm not about to teach you how to be a good loser; rather, I want to teach you how to think, play, and act like a winner, whether you come out on top or time ran out while you were still behind. Being a winner is a state of mind, both on and off the field.

For starters, respect your teammates, pick them up when they are down, and be thankful when they do the same for you. Respect your coaches, who volunteer their time and make tremendous sacrifices so you can have a positive soccer experience. Yes, you must respect referees too, because they have a critical, demanding job and do their best even when you'd swear they aren't watching the same game as you. Treating people as you would want to be treated is a good rule to live by, especially in the heat of battle when your temper threatens to take over.

Sportsmanship should be the bottom line no matter what the situation or score. You should never avoid shaking an opponent's hand after the game, even if you are hurting from the loss and the sharp kick to the shin she gave you in the closing minutes. Sportsmanship is being equally as gracious in defeat as in victory. When you win, never forget how the players on the other team are feeling, because we have all

If you don't respect the referee, you may find yourself
watching from the sidelines.

been on the other side of a 7–0 rout or have lost a heart-breaker in the final minutes on a penalty kick. As you feel the elation of victory, surely you must celebrate, but don't lose sight of your opponents, and whatever you do, don't rub it in. If you do, it will come back to haunt you, I promise.

I will never forget the aftermath of our agonizing semifinal defeat to Norway in the '95 World Cup. After the final whistle, the Norwegian players got on their hands and knees and formed a conga line, a kind of dancing human worm, that crawled around the field in celebration. It was easily the longest ten minutes of my soccer life, and I can assure you I haven't forgotten it because none of us looked away. We forced ourselves to watch through tear-filled eyes as Norway basked in the glory of their victory. We swore we'd never feel that way again and that the next time we met, it would be us in a pile of happy, sweaty bodies at the final whistle. Even though we later beat them en route to an Olympic Gold, we know they are the defending World Cup champs, and we still have a bone to pick with Norway.

That is not to say you shouldn't celebrate your victories and soccer's hardest task—scoring—with exuberance. For too long, society has imposed restrictions on girls and women, telling us that when we achieve something we are not supposed to show excitement and emotion. We are expected to go about it in a quiet, dignified way, be thankful, and not call attention to ourselves. It's time to break this stereotype of the passive woman, and one of the best ways I can think of to do this is to raise a ruckus when you stick the ball in the back of the net. Goals are so difficult to come by that when you get one, you should mark the occasion. Run with joy and salute the fans, sprint to the team bench and make a dogpile, do a little dance with the corner flag, a Shannon MacMillan slide on your stomach, a Tiffeny Milbrett dance, or a brisk jog for the TV cameras.

Tiffeny Milbrett shows off her signature jig after scoring a goal.

And yet individual heroics should never overshadow the pride you take in your team. Scoring three goals in a losing effort is no occasion to turn cartwheels. You must live and die with your team. If you see a team where every player has this attitude, you will see a team of winners.

To win on the field, your body needs every edge it can get off the field. That means eating good foods, staying hydrated by drinking water, juices, and sports drinks, and of course, avoiding drugs, alcohol, and cigarettes. Learning what foods work for you, how much rest your body needs, when you can push yourself to your limit, and what your limits are: These are the foundation for your hard work and training.

But after you've, say, run the stadium stairs, done your 40-yard sprints, and lifted weights for an hour (in other words, done a half-baked Carla Overbeck workout), remember to take time for yourself. The real winners have balance in their lives. When training camp gets too intense, I recommend doing what we do—goof off. That means playing hearts for Oreo cookies, cruising the local mall, and watching a tape of any Adam Sandler movie.

You can't stay focused on soccer all the time. It's just not healthy, and you risk burning yourself out. Having hobbies and other interests will keep you fresh, so that when you return to the field, you'll be relaxed and eager to play. My secret passion is golf. I love it, and whenever my schedule allows it, I hit the links with some friends and do my best to keep the ball in the fairways and out of the traps.

Being a winner is also pursuing your dream with energy and determination. I admire dreamers, people who set lofty goals and then go about trying to reach them. Set your goals high enough so that it takes effort to achieve them; the goals themselves are not as important as the simple fact that you have them and are striving to realize them.

You have to differentiate between big dreams and the attainable goals. Your ultimate dream may be to play for the U.S. Women's National Team. But in fact, very few do. So start with some reachable goals—playing for your high school team or your state Olympic Development team or winning a league championship, all great accomplishments. It is in the journey that you learn the most about yourself. That self-knowledge will help you not only along the way but also beyond, because of course, as you reach one goal, you gain confidence to aspire to the next.

I believe setting goals genuinely helps a person's growth and success, otherwise how can you really be sure what you are training for, why you're asking so much of yourself? Most people have a vague idea in their mind about the future, and that uncertainty impedes their ability to achieve greatness. Write your goals down or articulate them. This process will give you focus, help you determine whether those aspirations are really right for you or whether you need to set new ones. Setting out without a direction will lead you nowhere, and dreams without follow-through are just that—dreams.

I had no idea I would ever be where I am today, that people would ask me for my autograph and chant my name, that I would do TV commercials and actually get paid for kicking a ball. I started playing soccer because I enjoyed it. Each day I focused on the little things I needed to do to get better, and they led to bigger and bigger things. My goals when I hit my midteens were to play for North Carolina and then the National Team. As it turned out, I achieved them in reverse order. I made my National Team debut at fifteen and didn't enroll at UNC until two years later. When I entered the National Team environment and came to know what playing for your country was all about, it fueled my desire to achieve even more. While much has changed since the early years of my career, much has stayed the same as well. I still put in all the hard work and play the game because I love it, but now I have an opportunity to make it my job. I wake up every morning and I'm a soccer player, and that's a pretty cool feeling.

In the end, one of the most important parts of being a winner in life is being happy. A happy person makes those around them happy as well, and that is one of the greatest gifts of all. Make decisions in your life that lead to happiness, and that can be a lot more difficult than making decisions on the field that lead to goals. But like on the field, if you make a bad decision, you have to bounce back and try to make the next one better. I firmly believe that if you pursue what you love, you will find happiness. We all know that the pursuit will be filled with its share of hardships and struggles, but if I can follow my life's passion despite all the changes in schools, cities, and friends of my childhood, so can you.

After every game or practice, if you walk off the field knowing that you gave everything you had, you will always be a winner. This is an extremely difficult concept to embrace, as society certainly differentiates tremendously between winners and losers. But you must always believe in yourself and take satisfaction in the fact that you did everything in your power to help your team try to win. If you can learn to equate effort with success, you will be not only a winner on the field but, through that effort, a winner in life as well.

FOURTEEN

Champion of
the World

have always been uncomfortable talking about my personal accomplishments, but I must say that scoring my one hundredth career international goal was surprisingly emotional for me. When I really stop and think, I have to admit that I'm a bit in awe and even thankful for the opportunity to play enough times for my country that I could score so many goals. Before I bagged my hundredth, only two players in the history of soccer had scored one hundred or more goals, both Italian women. Legend Carolina Morace powered in 105 in her brilliant career, while Elisabetta Vignotto, who preceded Morace in the 1970s and 1980s, holds the world scoring record at 107. I became the first American to join that century club, but truth be told, Michelle Akers would have passed one hundred long before me had it not been for her battle against Chronic Fatigue Syndrome. Because of what Michelle has

The next time I get this emotional over a goal will be after burying number 108 for the world scoring record.

done for women's soccer, I wish she had reached one hundred before me, but of course, that has never stopped me from scoring as many goals as I can.

I didn't even know that I was getting close to one hundred until the Goodwill Games in July of 1998. I scored two goals against China in the championship game for numbers ninety-six and ninety-seven. We played Canada several days later, but I didn't score, and we didn't come together again until a month after that, in September, for the Nike U.S. Women's Cup. I scored two goals against Mexico in Boston during the first game of the tournament to bring me up to ninety-nine. By that time, Sammy Sosa and Mark McGwire had broken Roger Maris's home-run record and were battling each other for the all-time record. We headed to Rochester, New York, for our second game against Russia, and since I was "chasing history" as well, the media thought it would be a fun story to compare me with the two sluggers, which I thought was pretty funny. Somehow, I think the ball for my one hundredth goal will fetch a bit less than McGwire's three-million-dollar seventieth home-run ball. But still, the media attention added a certain excitement to the chase, and the night of the game, almost thirteen thousand people packed Frontier Field to capacity, creating an electric atmosphere. A guy in one end zone had a big sign that said MCGWIRE 63, SOSA 63, HAMM 99. That was pretty cool.

I had a chance to score in the first half but passed to Tiffeny Milbrett instead. She scored, which was awesome, because she was playing in her one hundredth game. Tiffeny repaid the favor later in the half with a beautiful cross from the left wing. A Russian defender misplayed the ball, and it bounced perfectly for me to roof a right-footed shot into the net from about 7 yards out.

If I didn't think goal number one hundred was going to be a big deal, when the ball went in the net the roar from the crowd certainly changed my mind. I was so excited all I could do was run. The players and coaches on the bench emptied onto the field, and everyone mobbed me as if I'd just scored the winning goal in the World Cup. Our captain, Carla Over-beck, presented me with the game ball, and the crowd stood and cheered for what seemed to me an embarrassingly long time. Despite my shyness, I've learned that I can't take these moments for granted. When my career is over, I'm sure I'll look back on that night with pride and nostalgia.

My one hundredth international goal will rank right alongside another memorable experience, one that took place not on the soccer field but on the basketball court at the University of North Carolina. No, I didn't dunk on fellow Tar Heel Michael Jordan in a game of one-on-one, but I did join him and a select group of athletes honored by having their jerseys retired by the university. The night took on some extra-special importance for me, because along with my number, Kristine Lilly's was retired as well.

For a school or team to retire your number is the ultimate compliment, and being there with Kristine made it even more emotional, if that's possible. Kristine and I joined the National Team at the same time, played our first international match together, went to the same college, and won three NCAA championships together.

My number, 19, and Kristine's, 15, were retired at halftime of a Duke vs. Carolina basketball game. Basketball is a huge social and sporting event in North Carolina to begin with, but when interstate rival Duke is the visiting team, the "Dean Dome" takes on the raucous trappings of a championship game. To have the ceremony at halftime of the Duke game underscored how much the university cared about us and our achievements.

Carolina is my home. I grew tremendously as a person and player in Chapel Hill, and if it wasn't for my Carolina experience, I definitely wouldn't be where I am today. When I walked out onto the court that night, the fans rose out of their seats and gave us a huge standing ovation. People clapped for what seemed like forever. Everything that I felt about UNC and its community came out that night, and Kristine and I were both choking back the tears. I'm proud to have helped bring home four NCAA titles and establish the program as one of the best in all of sports.

UNC's team in 1992, my junior year, was something to behold. We had a combination of players that clicked so well off the field that our bonding translated on the field into a devastating, unselfish attack. In terms of offense, it was probably the most dynamic team Anson has ever had, and that's saying a lot. Tisha Venturini was a sophomore and played in the midfield with Angela Kelly and Danielle Egan. We had Shelly Finger in goal and Zola Springer, Dawn Crow, Roz Santana, and Keri Sanchez in the back, all fast and rugged defenders. The forward line featured Kristine, Rita Tower, and me.

We all pushed one another to be better, and we achieved something in the NCAA championship game that will never be done again. We scored nine goals against Duke (yes, the hated Blue Devils), ironically after they had scored first, and won 9–1. It was Kristine Lilly's last college game, and even

Many have called our 4–3 overtime victory against NC State in the
quarterfinals of the 1989 NCAA National Championship tournament one of
the most exciting college games ever played. It was a war and I was one of
the casualties. Here, Linda Hamilton and Kristine Lilly help me
off the field after the game.

though I won another championship the next year as a senior, that NCAA title my junior year remains among my greatest triumphs on the soccer field.

The first-ever Women's World Cup was held in China in 1991 after FIFA, the world governing body of soccer, decided that women indeed deserved a World Cup of their own. Winning this groundbreaking event will always be special for many reasons, but one stands out above the rest—it was the beginning of everything we have accomplished. For the first time the world knew that there was something unique happening in American women's soccer.

Winning in '91 was so cool because back then we were like a bunch of neighborhood kids who got together and played for the love of the sport. Prior to leaving for China, we would tell people that we were going to the World Cup, and they'd smile and say, "Uh, that's nice." But they didn't really have a clue as to what we were talking about. We left on our journey to East Asia with a media entourage of three.

A World Cup for women was what we'd all dreamed about, and now we were on our way. When we arrived in China, we were treated like World Cup players, we stayed in a luxury hotel, and we played in front of huge crowds. I look back at that trip, and it seems like an eternity ago in terms of our sport. By winning that tournament, we kicked open the door for women's soccer and let in millions of girls who could now brag that American women were the best soccer players in the world.

As strange as it seems today, we accomplished those great things in almost complete anonymity as far as the United States was concerned. There were no TV crews or fans waiting for us at the airport when we returned, just several

After the 1991 Women's World Cup in China, American women could truly say they were the best in the world.

friends and U.S. Soccer Federation representatives. *Sports Illustrated* chose to note the historic victory with a tiny mention in its scorecard section, and newspapers across the country buried the story next to the tire ads in the back. No one offered us endorsements, money, or fame, and while we enjoy those things now, it's not why we play. Look back at the pictures of all the young faces on that 1991 team, awash with smiles, the glow of a world championship, and athletic glory in its purest form, and it becomes obvious why we play.

At the 1995 Women's World Cup in Sweden, we entered the tournament as defending champions and the favorites to repeat. When we lost to Norway in the semifinals, it was the lowest we would ever be. I've told you how we forced ourselves to watch the celebration and later vowed never to experience that feeling again.

At the Atlanta Olympics in 1996, we recommitted ourselves to that purity of purpose—love for the game—and convinced ourselves we were going to win the first Gold Medal ever awarded for women's soccer. From day one of our Olympic preparation, it was obvious that we had a powerful group, both mentally and physically. Because of that confidence and some truly selfless performances, we beat China, 2–1, in front of more than 76,000 fans. We had our Gold.

While I didn't score or get an assist, I played a part in both our goals, despite a bum ankle earned in a collision with the Swedish keeper in our second game. For our first goal, Kristine struck a long cross from the left wing and I sliced through several Chinese defenders in the penalty box to smack a volley just before the ball hit the ground. Chinese goalkeeper Goa Hong made a brilliant reaction save to push the ball off the left post, but Shannon MacMillan pounced on the rebound and buried her shot from close range. On the winning goal, I sprang Joy Fawcett with a pass down the right flank and she and Tiffeny Milbrett did the rest. Joy blazed past the Chinese defense and slotted a perfect pass for Tiffeny to knock in the winner.

It was a tough, physical game, and my ankle was killing me, as I'd sprained it pretty badly. Tony could see I was hurting, but he would have had to drag me kicking and screaming off the field if he had substituted me, and I think he knew that. In the final minute I did come out, so that one of our most respected veterans, Carin Gabarra, could earn a cap in the Olympic final. I still didn't want to come off—heck, I never want to come off—but Carin deserved to be on the field for such a historic moment.

My elation when the final whistle blew eclipsed any pain I was feeling as I sprinted onto the field with my teammates. Normally you'll see a team take a victory lap, waving

From the Texas rec league Sidewinders to Olympic gold medalist. Wow!

together at the crowd as they circle the field. Not us. We went bananas. After we had untangled our massive dogpile of bodies, we went running around in seven different directions. Joy and Carin grabbed the Stars and Stripes and ran like lunatics across a battlefield, while the rest of us took off leaping, screaming, and hugging one another whenever we crossed paths. It was insane. We celebrated for a full twenty minutes before we went back into the locker room to change into our sweats for the medal ceremony. Inside the locker room there were more hugs, tears, and a shared satisfaction that only teammates can have at such a special moment in their careers. We walked back out onto the field, and no one had left! It was still packed with people screaming for us! I remember limping up to the podium and taking my place between Michelle and Shannon and being overwhelmed by all the emotions swirling inside me: pride in the deafening chants of "USA, USA!," satisfaction in all the hard work my teammates and I had put in to get here, and no little amount of awe at the universal symbol of excellence, an Olympic Gold Medal, now hanging from my neck.

Let me tell you now that all those lessons I've shared—work harder than anyone else, take risks to be a winner, be a team player, celebrate your victories—will pay off whether or not you ever win a medal, Olympic or otherwise. If you go for the goal, like we do on the National Team, you'll always be reaching for a higher place. Each victory is great in and of itself, but champions are on a never-ending quest.

When we were walking off the field, all of us still hugging and smiling our world-champion smiles, Foudy reminded us that we weren't finished. "Okay, guys," she said, "now let's win back the World Cup!"

Afterword

Winning It All

The World Cup had been our focus, our mission, ever since we walked off the field nearly three years ago with our Olympic Gold Medals, and now as it drew near, the pressure to succeed was intense. The media had decided that anything less than victory on our home turf would be considered a failure. And even though this team thrives under pressure, we're still human and cherished the few opportunities to take our minds off of the upcoming tournament.

In early June, Nike honored me at its world headquarters in Beaverton, Oregon. I was thrilled to have my teammates as well as my family along at the ceremony where Nike dedicated a building to me. And not just a little shack either. This building is huge! They say if you stood the building on its side, it would measure 63 stories. Christiaan was there, too, but he had to leave for his assignment in Japan right after the ceremony and would miss seeing the World Cup in person. The Marines wait for no one!

To lighten the mood, my teammates, led by our equipment manager Dainis (ever the jokester), poked fun at the Mia Hamm Building. They plastered the equipment room at the hotel with strips of athletic tape, labeling everything from a lamp to an ice container the "Mia Hamm Something." There was the "Mia Hamm Lamp," the "Mia Hamm Air Conditioner," the "Mia Hamm Remote Control" and I believe there was a "Mia Hamm Toilet Seat" as well. Dainis even put a piece of tape on my jersey and called it the "Mia Hamm Mia Hamm Jersey."

Two days later we beat Canada, 4–2, on ABC in the first women's soccer game ever broadcast on network television. It was our last game before the World Cup opener at Giants Stadium in New Jersey. We took a week off and then regrouped for our final week of training before the biggest event of our lives. We were ready.

That week we held our pre–World Cup training camp at the Pingry School, a small private school in suburban New Jersey that had a big hill next to the practice field. The hill was covered with fans every training session. Everyone was focused, feeling fit and strong, and the competitive juices were flowing.

We also had a blast off the field. We had a whole floor to ourselves at our hotel, complete with a "player lounge," where we hung out talking, playing games, snacking, and watching TV and movies. Our sports psychologist Colleen Hacker and our assistant coach Lauren Gregg had made motivational videotapes for each of us, splicing together highlights of each player. We watched a few each night leading up to the first game. Julie and Tisha made one of the most hilarious home movies I've ever seen, spoofing Brandi's risqué photo shoot that she did for a magazine using the theme for *Austin Powers*, which was no doubt our "team movie" during the tournament. "Yeah, baby."

It was also that week that Brandi went on the *David Letterman Show* and Dave became smitten with the team. Dave decreed himself our official owner and said that if we needed anything, we should call him. We were officially dubbed "Babe City" by Dave and he just couldn't stop talking about us. In truth, throughout the tournament, it was a welcome distraction for us. It was better to answer questions from the media about Dave than to critique yourself and your team's performance every day.

We opened the Women's World Cup against Denmark on June 19, 1999. People forgot that while we were defending Olympic champions, we were not defending World Cup champions. That distinction belonged to Norway—they had taken it from us four years earlier in Sweden—and we wanted it back.

At the hotel before the game, we had an impromptu dance party in the hall of our floor. We were just a bunch of girls acting wacky, singing and trying to work off some of that nervous energy. Most of us painted our nails in some red, white, and blue design. Painting our nails seems to be a tradition for us during big tournaments. We couldn't wait to kick off this thing.

The first game was magical. We drove to Giants Stadium

with a police escort because the traffic was clogged for miles. We had heard several days before that the game would probably be a sell-out; it still didn't prepare us for the wild scene that greeted us in the stadium parking lot.

There were thousands of people with their faces painted, waving flags, holding balloons, wearing our jerseys and carrying signs. When they saw the bus, they went crazy. I'll never forget the expressions on their faces when they glanced up and saw us looking back. For the first time, we felt as if the whole nation was behind us.

I don't remember who was sitting next to me on the bus. We sat two to a seat and everyone was intense and focused. Some had headphones on and listened to music, while others just stared out the windows, trying to psyche themselves up. But I do remember looking in all my teammates' eyes and sharing an unspoken understanding of how this was in some way the end of our long journey. We didn't need to say a word to share memories of all the ups and downs, all the training, the travel, the thousands of hotel rooms, and the competition all over the world during the past decade that had prepared us for this moment. As the bus rolled into the stadium parking lot, I remembered the times when fans only called us by our numbers and not our names. I remembered the times before we had websites dedicated to us, before we got fan mail by the bushel, and before our games were on TV. Sitting there on the bus I realized that the difference between the past and the present was night and day. And this day was going to be a great one.

When we walked out on the field for pregame warm-ups, 78,000 friends roared as one. Usually during pregame, we are running back and forth, high-fiving each other, pumping up each other. But before this game, we didn't need to get pumped. We just hugged each other. It was like we had achieved something we had worked for our whole lives and the game hadn't even started yet!

I'd like to say that I was more excited than nervous, but it wouldn't be true. I was one of the players who was supposed to lead our team, the one who was supposed to score the goals. I felt a lot of pressure, but I also felt a certain calmness, because I knew that if I fell down, there were 19 other players, three coaches and a great support staff to pick me up. We were going to do it together.

When the game started, all that nervous energy had to be kept in check. We didn't want to exhaust ourselves in the first 10 minutes. We did our best to stay calm, and after 17 minutes, I found an opening. Brandi looped a pass into the right side of the penalty box. I ran onto the ball as the Danish defender closed me down, but I popped it over her head. I let it bounce and hit a half-volley that sailed into the roof of the net at the near post. The stadium exploded! Well, it sounded like it anyway.

I turned and ran back to midfield, where I leapt into the open arms of Carla and Joy. We joked about it later that the defenders never get to celebrate because they are always so far back when the ball goes into the net, so I was happy that they were the first players I hugged. I kept saying, "Are you kidding me! Are you kidding me!"

The goal reminded me of when I broke the all-time goal record back in April in a game against Brazil. When I scored my 108th goal it was exhilarating because my family was there and my teammates were all so proud of me. Everybody was celebrating and cheering then, but this was even better because it was the first step toward winning the World Cup. The goal gave the whole team confidence, and we started knocking the ball around a lot better.

In the second half, Julie brought down one of my crosses and scored a great goal that hit the underside of the crossbar and bounced down over the line. Then Kristine scored a well-deserved goal right at the end of the game on a fantastic shot from the top of the penalty box. It was extra-special for Kristine, who is from nearby Connecticut and is a HUGE fan of the New York Jets, who play their home games in that stadium.

We had delivered an impressive 3–0 victory in front of the largest crowd ever to watch a women's sporting event. We were off and running toward our destiny.

The next day, we traveled from New Jersey to Chicago for our second first-round game. It was against Nigeria, which marked the first time we had ever played an African team. We knew it would be a big test, especially since Nigeria had opened their tournament with a 2–1 win over North Korea.

We trained way out in the suburbs, about 45 minutes from Soldier Field. After the sell-out at Giants Stadium, you could tell that the momentum was really picking up. We started to have problems with fans at our hotel. Kids would bang on our doors and run away, call our rooms and leave us notes. One time the phone rang in my hotel room. "Hello?" I said. "Yeah . . . umm . . . is this Mia?" a young girl said at the other end. "Yes, this is Mia . . ." I said. "You are so awesome!!!!" Then she hung up. How she got through to my room, I don't know, because we were under aliases the whole time, but where there's a will, there's a way. And our fans have a lot of will! We signed and posed as much as we could, especially for the kids, but the craziness had just begun.

We had five days between the Denmark and Nigeria games, and each day, the number of fans coming to watch practice multiplied. There were fans of all ages and sizes. Daughters with dads, older people, students, coaches, little kids. The buzz at training was fun and we always had to wade through a sea of autograph seekers to get back to the bus. The media corps grew as well, and some of us were spending 30 to 45 minutes after practice in our tented-off area for interviews. The attention we were receiving was amazing and it fueled the public's passion for the team and the tournament.

The only time the media became burdensome was when everyone wanted to do one-on-one interviews and features with me. I made it known from the beginning that even though I usually got the most attention, I didn't want the Women's World Cup to be the "Mia Hamm Show." And, besides, I put so much pressure on myself, I don't need others doing it as well.

Soldier Field, like Giants Stadium, was sold out. Chicago is a great sports town and the intimacy of that stadium combined with 65,000 fans made it the loudest venue we played in. It was a night game, so the dew on the grass made the ball move a little bit quicker and the lights added a bit of a surreal feeling to the evening. The place went absolutely nuts when we walked onto the field for the national anthems. I remember thinking that we had arrived at our sport's pinnacle. Then, the game began.

Once again, we started out jittery and we had a couple of breakdowns, one of which led to Nigeria scoring just two minutes into the game. The crowd was in shock and the Nigerians were dancing up a storm, no doubt with images of one of the greatest upsets in women's soccer history dancing in their heads. But we didn't panic. We had 88 minutes left to play. We regrouped, refocused, and as it turned out scoring early might have been Nigeria's biggest mistake!

They were a tremendously athletic and talented team, but we knew we had the edge in experience and sophistication. And during a five-minute span starting in the 19th minute, those qualities helped us explode for three goals.

The first came when I bent a free-kick into the middle from the left wing. Michelle made a hard run to the near post and at first it looked like she deflected the ball into the net, even though it was later ruled that the Nigerian defender had kicked it into her own goal. Still, Michelle's presence had somehow forced that ball in, we were tied 1–1, and on our way to tying a U.S. record for the most goals scored in a Women's World Cup game. Just one minute later I took a pass down the right wing from Kristine, cut toward the goal, and absolutely pounded a shot underneath the crossbar that Nigeria goalkeeper Ann Chiejine had no chance to save. Once again, electricity raced through my body as I ran and slid in front of the bench. Carla came sliding in right after me and nailed me in the side with her knee. Ouch! But it would be one of the softer hits I took in that game, let me tell you.

Three minutes after my goal, Tiffeny Milbrett slammed in a shot from close range that Chiejine got her hand on but couldn't turn away. Kristine added a header from my corner kick in the 32nd minute, Michelle scored off a header in the 39th minute (they couldn't take that one away from her!) and then Brandi and Cindy combined on a beautiful double-header for our sixth goal of the half! We scored on five straight shots! It was raining goals!

Nigeria didn't just sit and watch, though. Instead, they punished us physically for the rest of the game. I got brutally fouled from behind several times and I got cleated in my stomach once. Julie almost had her leg broken on the sidelines and several other players got hammered. Nigeria actually had 29 fouls in the match to only three for us. But one thing that we can be proud of (besides the fact that we came out with no serious injuries) was that we never retaliated when it would have been easy to take a shot at one of them. We kept our cool—"ice" as we call it—and let our play decide the game.

While our team had a 6–1 lead at halftime, Tony took out Kate Sobrero, who was playing on a very sore ankle, and Michelle, who needed to rest as much as possible. I started the second half, but six minutes in, I got fouled hard again and Tony took me out, replacing me with Shannon MacMillan. Tiffeny added another goal in the 83rd minute to give the fans something else to yell about, and the game finished in a blur of flashbulbs and screaming kids. We took our lap around the field to show our appreciation for the fans and it was so loud I could barely hear the player jogging next to me.

We had one first-round game left to play and only two days to rest before facing North Korea. After getting beat up by the Nigerians, we needed every minute. Some of the starters didn't even practice the next day when we got to Boston. Tony told the press that a lot of the players were "knocked up," which the media thought was pretty funny. He meant that we were a bit bruised, and he was right.

The game at Foxboro was the first that wasn't sold out

and the media asked if we were disappointed. Disappointed with 50,000 fans watching us? Are you kidding? Maybe the media had forgotten the days when we played in front of 500, but we certainly hadn't. We were never going to take any of this for granted.

Foxboro was rocking as well, but the North Koreans didn't play a wide-open game like the Nigerians; instead they bunkered and played defense, and forced us to find a way through them.

Tony chose to rest some of the starters, giving the nod to Tiffany Roberts, Sara Whalen, Shannon MacMillan and Tisha Venturini. Michelle and Kate didn't play at all while Tiffeny and Julie Foudy came off the bench.

North Korea played with five defenders and we struggled to find space in our offensive third. The game was tied 0–0 at halftime, and both the crowd and our team seemed to be getting restless. But we were patient and knew that sometimes it takes time to wear down a team. We just kept chipping away and six minutes into the second half, Shannon, our "super sub," sliced across the top of the penalty box and directed a rocket into the lower left corner. Then, in front of the world, Shannon executed her trademark headfirst slide celebration and we piled on.

Shannon then set up Tisha for two beautiful head goals in the 68th and 76th minutes. We all know Tisha is one of the best headers in the world, but I was the only one who knew that she could do a back flip! Her first goal was an awesome diving header, but after her second, in which she out-jumped a defender to nod the ball home, she ran to the sideline and executed a round-off and a back flip that would have made Mary Lou Retton proud! It became one of the more memorable images of the World Cup. I'd give her a 10 easy. I'd seen her do it on the golf course before when she was just messing around, but no one on the bench knew that she took gymnastics when she was little, so they enjoyed it that much more.

With the 3–0 win, we clinched first place in our group and a meeting with Germany in the quarterfinals at Jack Kent Cooke Stadium outside Washington, D.C. It was a homecoming of sorts for me since I went to a year of high school in Virginia, so it was definitely nice to be back in an area where I was considered a "hometown" girl. Of course for me, a bunch of cities could claim that title since I moved around so much as a kid.

Actually, we were about ten seconds away from playing Brazil in the quarterfinals because Germany was ahead of Brazil 3–2 in injury time during their first-round game. But Brazil scored with almost no time left and tied the game, which gave them the group title and allowed them to avoid us in the quarters. Every game from here on was do-or-die.

Up to that point in the tournament, we found different ways to win each game. The first game we beat Denmark because we were the better team, both technically and tactically. Nigeria was an extremely athletic team and very attack-oriented, but we beat them because we were more experienced. The third game against North Korea was a mental test. We beat them psychologically by being patient and not getting frustrated.

The Germany game would be won on emotion.

We knew that we had played well in the tournament so far, but we also knew we could play better and all of us were ready to make the final three games of the tournament our strongest. But first we had to get through one of the best teams Germany had ever put together.

And then, two days before the game, I got injured.

I pulled my left hip flexor. It's a big sprinting muscle, one that helps lift your leg to run, and it hurt. It was uncomfortable to accelerate and, of course, acceleration is a big part of my game. I just didn't warm up enough at the beginning of training and then we jumped into a drill that was pretty dynamic right at the start. I felt it pull and it wasn't the same for the rest of the World Cup. The last thing you ever want is an injury that you are thinking about the entire game. It causes you to play a little more cautiously so you don't hurt yourself even worse, and that's not a good thing when you need to go all out against one of the best teams in the world. It was frustrating because it was a totally preventable injury. I should have simply taken some more time to warm up. But I didn't, I pulled it, and now I would have to suck it up for the rest of the tournament.

More than 50,000 fans, including President Clinton, Hillary, and Chelsea (I guess the ESPN commercials that challenged him to come worked!), jammed into Jack Kent Cooke Stadium, a beautiful, ultra-modern facility that serves as home to my favorite NFL team, the Washington Redskins. But early on, our fortunes went the way of the Redskins in recent years. In other words, we almost blew it in the first five minutes.

Brandi ran down a long through ball in the right side of the penalty box with little pressure on her back. It was a play that happens all the time in soccer. This time however, Brandi and Briana had a slight miscommunication and Bri rushed out of her goal as Brandi tried to tap it back for her to clear with her feet. The ball rolled by Bri, and rolled and rolled and rolled. Bri and Carla gave chase, but to no avail. It seemed like it was happening in slow motion, until the ball trickled over the line for an own goal. We were down 1–0 in a knockout game in the World Cup on a goal we had scored on ourselves.

Carla went up to Brandi and looked her straight in the eyes, and told her to forget about the mistake right now and that we had 85 minutes left to play. We just needed to score twice. Eleven minutes later, we got one. We pulled even after Michelle's shot rebounded off a German defender to Tiffeny, who stuck her shot into the left corner. Now we had the momentum. But the Germans were the last team to roll over and hand us the game.

Just before the half, Germany struck again. Their attacking midfielder Bettina Weigmann got a ball on the right side of the field, beat her defender inside, and cracked a shot that sailed into the side netting at the left post. We went into the locker room down a goal, again.

At halftime the mood in the locker room was more of annoyance than anything else. We had allowed ourselves to get into a hole not once, but twice. How frustrating! Those who really know the lighter side of Julie Foudy also know she has an intense side. We saw the latter in the locker room. Each player sat in a locker stall and I saw a mixture of shock, anger, and desire wash over everyone's faces. Julie went around to each player and with a cool stare said, "We are NOT losing this game. We didn't come this far to lose now. This is OUR tournament." Well, those weren't her exact words, I left a few of the more impassioned ones out, but you get the idea. Carla was also a calming influence in the locker room. Just her body language and demeanor alone gave us confidence that things would be all right. She didn't look panicked at all. She looked like a woman who was about to go out on the field and make things right again.

Tony told us that we had 45 minutes left of our dream and that we had to make the most of it. So we did. It took us just four minutes from the time the whistle blew to start the second half to tie the game. That was when we knew for sure that we weren't going to let our dreams die. Not that day.

In an amazing twist of fate, it was Brandi who scored the equalizer. On a corner kick from the left side, a German defender headed the ball back into the middle instead of away and Brandi pounced on the rebound, hitting a half-volley off the right post and in. The look on her face after the ball bounced down in the goal was one of the best moments of the World Cup. Equal parts relief, disbelief, and ecstasy all rolled into one ponytailed package.

The game was ours now and everyone on the field felt that we were going to win. We didn't know how, but we would find a way. That way came in the 66th minute from Shannon and Joy.

With Shannon waiting to come into the game at midfield, we got a corner kick and the substitution was made. Tiffeny was ready to take the corner, but when Shannon is in the game, she takes all the corner kicks, so Tiffeny waved her over. Shannon hits one of the best dead balls in the world and this one was perfect. She drove the ball on a line to the near post where Joy jumped and redirected the ball into the net just inside the post. German goalkeeper Silke Rottenberg flew in the air, but the ball was already stretching the back of the net.

Pandemonium broke loose on the field! In a matter of 21 minutes, we had come from a goal down to take the lead and Shannon was probably in the game for about 30 seconds when we scored. Talk about a "super sub!" It was her first touch of the game. It was extra-special for Shannon and Joy because they lived together in residency camp leading up to the World Cup, and Shannon has been Joy's number-one baby-sitter for Katey and Carli for a long time. I'm sure the girls were proud of both their mom and their best friend! (Later, someone asked Katey who her favorite player was and she said Shannon!)

The rest of the match was fast and tense, with the Germans fighting for a spot in the semis. But Briana stepped up and made four saves in the last 18 minutes, including one in stoppage time, and now *we* were in the semifinals. The roar at the final whistle was deafening and several German players slumped to the turf in disbelief. Both teams gave everything they had. We were emotionally spent, but the adrenaline was rushing as we took our thank-you lap for the fans. We knew it was one of the greatest victories in our history and the drama of the game definitely raised the level of enthusiasm for the tournament that had been snowballing since the opener.

After the game, President Clinton visited our jubilant locker room. It was kind of crazy seeing him just walk in with Hillary and Chelsea. He was smiling from ear-to-ear and he told us how proud we should be, not only for our performance in the game but also for the way we had captured America's hearts. It was really cool. We chatted with him and his family and snapped tons of photos, and then he went around the room and shook each player's hand to personally congratulate her. What a night!

After the Germany game, all the right things were said, which was important for us. Tony told us that we had won the game on heart and we knew we had played the best German team we'd seen in a long time. Not only that, but Germany played their best game and for us to come back when we were down was an important hurdle for us.

The next day we traveled to the Bay Area to prepare for the semifinal and did something we rarely do—we took a chartered plane. The U.S. Soccer Federation footed the bill and let me tell you, it's the only way to fly! Every seat was in first class, there was tons of leg room, and more snacks than you could ever eat on one cross-country flight. I can see why all the NBA teams do it. Not having to deal with a commercial flight was a huge benefit to us in preparing for the semifinal because after that travel day, we had just one day before facing Brazil at Stanford Stadium, and the time we spent on the plane was relaxing and fun as opposed to spending it stressing about the next game.

Brazil had played another amazing match, defeating Nigeria, 4–3, in sudden death overtime after being ahead 3–0! A spectacular free-kick by Sissi put the Brazilians into the semifinals. Heading into the game, both teams would no doubt be tired from traveling and from exerting so much energy and emotion in their quarterfinal victories.

I think all the players would say that the Brazil game was the most nerve-racking of the tournament, because everyone wants desperately to make it to the Final when you get that close. We matched up well against Brazil, but they had incredibly talented attackers who could decide a game with one touch.

But we were confident because in the months leading up to the Cup, we had beaten them twice in a row by 3–0 scores. We felt that if we could put enough pressure on them that we would have a good chance to win. Sure enough, Brazil made the first mistake.

For a change, we struck first. Five minutes into the game, Julie sent a cross from the left side. Brazil's goalkeeper Maravilha leaped for the ball, but it glanced off her gloves and Cindy Parlow was Cindy-on-the-Spot to head the ball home.

A goal like that can really rattle a team. But while it frustrated Brazil a bit, they bounced back and played very well, especially in the second half. Brazil is a great team and they were the first in the tournament to out-shoot us (13–10 for the game). If it wasn't for Briana, we would have been playing for third place.

She made four spectacular saves during the game and dominated the air in the penalty box. In the first half, she snuffed Pretinha from point-blank range. In the second half, she made two brilliant reaction saves and dove backward to tip another over the crossbar, preserving our precarious 1–0 lead.

In the 80th minute, I finally got a little bit of space down the left wing and raced toward the goal. As I neared the penalty box, I got clipped from behind and crashed hard to the ground. Was I in the penalty box? Yes! Penalty kick! I had gained a half-step on Brazil's central defender Elane, but she had stuck her hip into my leg and grabbed my shoulder. There was no doubt who would take it.

Michelle stepped up and calmly drilled her shot into the

corner, just like she had done in the semifinals of the '96 Olympics against Norway (although that one was to tie the game). I was so happy for her because it was just so appropriate that she would score such an important goal. We had a 2–0 lead with 10 minutes to play and there was NO WAY we were going to let Brazil back into the game. The final whistle blew and we were in the World Cup Final!

What a relief! We had made the Final and now we would have five days to rest before playing the biggest game of our lives. The week of preparation was very calm, focused, and relaxed despite the circus that was going on around us. During that week, Tom Brokaw had come to our practice to interview us, as did Robin Roberts from ABC and ESPN, as well as reporters from all over the country and all over the world. At our final open practice at Pomona-Pitzer College there were hundreds of kids, and we needed a police motorcycle escort just to get through the crowds to the field. When the kids saw us, they started screaming as if we were rock stars or something. It was wild.

Two days before the Final, I was riding down in the elevator to one of our team meals. I was one of the last ones down and wasn't really paying attention when all of a sudden the door opened and there was Christiaan! I leaped into his arms and hugged him tight. It was a huge surprise. All of my teammates were waiting to see the reunion because they knew I would walk out of the elevator any minute. Somehow Christiaan had gotten permission to come and taken a military transport to southern California. It was great to have him there. It really helped me relax and take my mind off the game in the two days before the Final.

The capacity of the Rose Bowl for the Final was supposed to be around 83,000, but the demand for tickets was so great that the organizers opened up an additional 7,000 seats. They were snapped up in a matter of hours and amazingly, five days before the game, the Rose Bowl was sold out. But I guess it wasn't amazing, because by then the tournament had taken on a life of its own, transcending a sporting event and developing into a cultural phenomenon.

One of my favorite pictures from the World Cup was a big group photo of all the staff and players together taken in the locker room before the Final. We all had our arms around each other and you can feel the closeness of the team from looking at that photo. You look at all our faces and you don't see any sign of stress or tension, just big smiles. To play in such a big game and be able to enjoy every moment without being completely stressed out made it even more of a wonderful experience. We had made the Final and we were really having a great time, which is what this sport is all about.

On July 10, 1999, we stepped onto the field at the Rose Bowl to face off against China for the World Cup Final in what was one of the greatest moments of my career. I was nervous, the team was nervous, but the 90,185 screaming, face-painted, flag-waving fans that packed the Rose Bowl to the rims didn't seem to notice. They were just excited to be there. Very few thought a women's sporting event could draw such a crowd, including us. It was a proud moment for everyone, from the players to the organizers to the fans to all the people involved in girls and women's soccer across the country.

We couldn't let them down.

But then we ran into the Great Wall of China. Boy (or

should I say girl), were they tough. The one thing that you had in that game was tremendous effort for 120 minutes from two great defensive teams. Perhaps that kind of a game was unexpected because both China and the United States are attack-oriented teams. But whether it was total respect for the opposition's attack and their personalities, or the pressure of a World Cup Final, both teams played a defensive game.

Still, it was as an exciting 0–0 match as they come, since both teams were working their butts off to get a goal and at the same time so focused on not letting the other team score! We took only 10 shots during regulation and China had seven. Michelle had to come out of the game at the end of regulation when Briana accidentally smacked her in the head when they both jumped for a high ball in the penalty box. Michelle had left it all on the field on the hot day. She had to be helped to the locker room for treatment. Sara Whalen replaced her for the sudden-death overtime, or as FIFA calls it, "Golden Goal."

As the overtime started, the tension got even thicker. Admittedly, China took the game to us in the first 15-minute period. One thing I hope people never forget is that in the one hundredth minute we were inches from losing, literally. I hope history doesn't gloss over the fact that if Kristine Lilly hadn't headed the ball off the goal line, the World Cup trophy would be in Beijing right now.

It was on a corner kick from the left side and Chinese defender Fan Yunjie leaped over several of our defenders and sent a header toward the goal and over Briana. Let me say that again—"over" Briana. My stomach flip-flopped. It's amazing to think that you can run through the gamut of emotions in a split-second, but that's what happened. Total horror to total relief to total joy. Kristine headed the ball down and it hit the flying Bri on its way out. Brandi came in with a flying side-volley clear to get the ball out of danger and the entire stadium let out a collective sigh of relief.

With that scare behind us, we had more control of the game in the second overtime period. As they ran at us relentlessly in the first overtime, I was praying for penalty kicks. Then, when we outplayed them in the second, I was thinking that we were going to end it. But then the final whistle blew. The 1999 Women's World Cup title would be decided from the penalty spot.

I'll share a secret with you. I'm not good at penalty kicks. Some players can take them. I can't. I've always struggled. As we were getting ready for the shoot-out, getting our legs rubbed, drinking water, and pumping each other up, Lauren Gregg made the order for the penalties. I would be shooting fourth.

I went up to Shannon, who had come into the game midway through the second half for Cindy, and asked her if she was one of the first to shoot. She wasn't. I asked her if she wanted to be. She did. So I went over to Lauren and told her that maybe Mac should be taking the kick. She told me that I had to have confidence and that I would be all right.

As we lined up at midfield, I was yelling and pumping up my teammates. So were the fans, who filled the stadium, the parking lot around the stadium, the highway next to the parking lot, and every neighborhood for miles around with chants of U-S-A, U-S-A.

China shot first, and scored.

Carla would shoot first for us.

Carla is our captain for a good reason. She leads through voice and action. She's always intense on the field and she's always there to encourage us in a positive way. She wasn't going to let us down. So when she stepped up to take the first penalty, I knew she would get us off to a good start.

Taking penalties is never easy, but the first one is tough because you don't want to put your team in a mental hole—or behind on the scoreboard—right away. The thing I remember the most is that everyone was decisive and everyone had a certain confidence about them when they walked up there to take the kick. Carla walked up to the ball like she owned the stadium and stuck it. What a way to start!

China made their second kick and then it was Joy's turn. She kind of wrongfooted Hong Goa, China's great goalkeeper, and buried her shot in the opposite corner.

Liu Ying from China stepped up to take the third kick. Briana has said that she had a feeling that this would be the one. She said she could see it in her body language. Liu shot, but Briana fully extended to her left and batted the ball away. The stadium, and I'm sure the 40 million watching on TV, went bonkers! We had our opening.

Kristine shot next. I remember standing at midfield during the shoot-out and talking to Lil. She said that Goa was diving to our left, which is where Lil wanted to put her kick. But Lil said that if she put the ball where she wanted it, Goa wouldn't stop it even if she guessed correctly. Goa did, but it didn't matter. Kristine just planted it in the back of the net! It was probably the best of the five, just totally unstoppable. She says that she was trying to hit it on the ground, but she hit it perfectly, right into the upper corner. We had a 3–2 lead after three kicks each.

China made their fourth kick and then it was my turn.

I would like to tell you what happened on my kick, but I really don't remember. All I know is that as I was walking up to the ball I was doing my best not to throw up. Okay, I wasn't that nervous, but I was close. I've seen it on tape, and I remember jogging up there and getting the ball, but I don't remember anything after that. Pretty weird, huh? I guess in a situation like that, your natural instincts just take over. Luckily, my instincts were good enough and I rolled my shot into the right corner to put us up 4–3 after four kicks each.

Sun Wen shot fifth for China and buried her shot. It was now up to our fifth shooter—Brandi—to win the Women's World Cup.

I knew when Brandi walked up to the ball that we were going to win. She kicked it perfectly, just inside the right post, and in an instant, every emotion I ever felt, and some I never even knew existed, filled me. As we sprinted toward Brandi, I felt as if I were flying across the field. I couldn't even feel the field under my cleats. I was running toward Brandi, but then I veered off and went to jump on Bri. The whole time I was sprinting I was saying to myself, "I just can't believe this."

The celebration on the field after the game was a blur of tears, screams, hugs, and confetti that rained down on us. We did our "We're going to Disneyland!" commercial, got our medals on stage and received the trophy from FIFA president Sepp Blatter and Women's World Cup president Marla Messing. The whole crowd was basking in the achievement, which was appropriate because they were as important to the event as we were. I was crying for most of the time. The emotions you experience when you've achieved something that you've really worked your whole life for are impossible to describe. And to do it with a group of women who are as close to me as sisters made it all the more sweeter.

When we finally got back into the locker room, it was packed with people. Then President Clinton came in (that's twice he visited us in the locker room!) and said how we had given everyone in America a great gift, and how the whole country was proud of what we had done.

We held our post-game press conference in front of the hundreds of journalists who came from all over the world to cover the game and answered as many questions as we possibly could. I told everyone how grateful I was to my family for supporting me through the years and how much I loved my teammates. It was the time of our lives.

For China, it was a different story. For every winner, of course, there is a loser, and none of us who were at the last World Cup could forget what it was like being in the losing locker room. I had heard that China wanted to exchange jerseys, but everything was so crazy right after the game that it was hard to do. So once things settled down a bit, I went over to their locker room. I asked one of their staff members if I could go in and they brought me inside. The Chinese players were sitting by their stalls, with their heads hanging down. I spotted Sun Wen and walked over to her. I handed her my jersey, and through her broken English, my two words of Chinese, and the interpreter, I told her that I thought she was the best player in the World Cup.

I got back to my locker room and finally showered. That's when the adrenaline wore off and I crashed. Literally. I collapsed right there in the locker room.

Our medical staff pumped three liters of fluids into me

intravenously, but it didn't make me feel any better. My team-mates and family helped me back to my room, and I have to say I have never felt worse in my life. Anything I tried to do to get comfortable only made it hurt more. Lying down hurt. Sitting up hurt. Having my eyes open hurt. Having my eyes closed hurt. In case it isn't clear, I was in pain. I was also really hungry and I tried to eat and drink, but I couldn't keep any-thing down. I couldn't talk. It was a combination of severe dehydration and just being physically and emotionally spent. My body just shut down.

I wanted to go to the post-game party at a hotel in Pasadena, but I couldn't even get out of bed. That was disap-pointing because I really wanted to go out and celebrate with the people I'd spent the last six or seven months with. Heck, I'd spent the last 10 years with them. And here I was asleep by 8 o'clock.

The next morning, it still felt as if there was an elephant standing on my head, but at least now it was a small elephant. I felt like I hardly slept at all, when I had really been out cold for 12 hours. Luckily, I got some sleep because the next 36 hours were going to be crazy.

We had to be at Disneyland at 9 A.M. We had a victory parade through the park, rolling down the streets on two floats with Goofy and Mickey and a whole bunch of other Disney characters. Then we had a rally in another part of the park, did more interviews, and then shot the cover of *People* magazine. Of all the covers we were on, that was my favorite because we were all together.

From Disneyland we went to the Los Angeles Conven-tion Center for another rally. There were tons of people there, too, and lines of TV cameras. Julie emceed the whole event. She was hilarious as always introducing everyone. What touched me the most was how grateful everyone was for the memorable ride we took them on during the last three weeks. They were just yelling, "Thank you! Thank you!" Fathers were thanking us for what we did for their daughters, and daughters were thanking us for what we did for their fathers!

From the Los Angeles Convention Center, we went straight to the airport to catch a flight to New York, where we were scheduled to do *Good Morning America* and the *Today Show* the next day. Except our flight was delayed. We went to a hotel near the airport, had an oh-so-glamorous dinner of cheeseburgers and french fries, and crashed on the floor of the executive lounge until it was time to go.

We finally got on the plane in Los Angeles around 7:30 P.M., but didn't get to Newark airport until 3:30 in the morning. No one could believe what happened next. We had a police escort to our hotel in New York, as if there were a lot of traffic at 4 A.M. It's great to be world champions.

When we got to the hotel, my roommate Shannon and I just fell on our beds the minute we walked into our room. But by now it was 5:30 and we had to be in the lobby at 6 A.M. so when I lay down, I was like, "Who are we kidding? It's going to hurt even more waking up in 30 minutes." So we just got dressed in our matching Ann Taylor outfits (we were exhausted, but we looked good!) and at 6 A.M. we went over to *Good Morning America*. They surprised us by having track legend Jackie Joyner-Kersee in the studio, who is one of my heroes, and then Wayne Gretzky and Vice President Al Gore called in to congratulate us. And it wasn't even 8 A.M. yet! Then we jumped on a bus and scooted over to the *Today Show*. We did that show outside, and it was like a carnival with everybody cheering and waving and holding posters. Then we hopped back on the bus and went over to the CNN studios and finally to Fox. The papers the next day had photos of us under headlines U.S. WOMEN TAKE NEW YORK!

They should have read U.S. WOMEN COLLAPSE FROM EXHAUSTION AND SLEEP FOR EIGHT HOURS IN NEW YORK. Some players left for home that afternoon, but a group of us stayed, took a long nap, and went out for a night on the town. We had a blast, even though we had to put up with a posse of reporters and photographers who were following us around. Who did they think we were, the Spice Girls? I guess women's soccer has truly arrived when we have paparazzi stalking us!

The next morning we had a rally outside Niketown. They closed off a street for the event, and it was overflowing with our fans. Even Donald Trump was there! Of course, the rally was right outside Trump Tower. Julie spoke (and thanked Donald for that extra million he was giving each player—she's so funny) and then *Sports Illustrated* presented Brandi with the framed cover of her issue. Women's soccer on the cover of *Sports Illustrated*! And the famous sports bra celebration shot, no less! She was also on the cover of *Newsweek* and *Time*. We were the second story in history to be on the cover of *People*, *Newsweek*, *Time*, and *Sports Illustrated* in the same week.

The next day, several of us went to the WNBA All-Star Game. They introduced our team at a timeout and we got a standing ovation from a sold-out Madison Square Garden crowd. The WNBA players even took a break from their huddle and clapped. Then we went up to a luxury box to say hello to Tipper Gore (we had met her at a Women's World Cup function earlier in the year at her house in Washington, D.C.) and Jane Pauley was there, too. I think they were as excited to meet us as we were to meet them!

The following Sunday, eight days after we had won, we all met in Washington, D.C. This time we were going to see the President instead of the other way around.

Even though we felt a little like Forrest Gump—"We're going to meet the President, again"—going to the White House was pretty special. We were given a quick tour and I was just hoping that we wouldn't break anything since our team can get pretty crazy. But we managed to avoid knocking over any of those antiques that belonged to George Washington, and then we took part in a wonderful ceremony on the South Lawn. I heard that President Clinton, Hillary, Tipper, and Al Gore rearranged their schedules so that they could all speak. It was boiling hot, but it didn't matter, we were all just honored to be there.

We went back to the hotel for a few hours and then hopped on a bus to Andrews Air Force Base, which is where they keep the presidential fleet of planes. We had been invited to go to the launch of the space shuttle at Cape Canaveral in Florida. It was the first ever shuttle flight commanded by a woman, so it seemed appropriate for us to go, and besides, how often do you get to see a space shuttle launch in person? But we had no way of getting down there . . . until Hillary invited us to fly with her and Chelsea.

So there we were on Air Force 3 (we figured Al Gore's plane was Air Force 2) when Kristine and I were invited to go in the cockpit and strap in for takeoff! Could we be having MORE fun?

We landed at Cape Canaveral in the middle of the night (the launch was scheduled for around 12:30 A.M.) and were ushered to a VIP area which provided a great view. Unfortunately, the launch was aborted for a technical problem, which happens from time to time. Still, the whole experience was awesome nonetheless.

We said goodbye to Hillary and Chelsea and took two corporate jets back to New York courtesy of AFLAC Insurance and FedEx. We got to New York in the wee hours of the morning, again, but hey, we were used to it by then.

The next day we did some shopping, and then we all hopped on a bus to go see Dave. David Letterman that is. It was a big thrill for the whole team to do the show and we got a chance to thank Dave for all his support during the tournament.

While we were waiting to go on, Brandi dragged out a box with replica national team jerseys for all of us, except with our nicknames on the back instead of our last names. She got them for all of the staff as well. It was such a nice thing to do.

Brandi and I sat in the coveted chairs next to Dave's desk and chatted away, but the whole team paraded out at the end of the show with the trophy. They dropped balloons and confetti and it was a great way to end the magical post-victory tour.

But it wasn't over yet! We hopped back on the bus and hightailed it over to the Continental Airlines arena because Marla Messing had gotten us VIP tickets to see Bruce Springsteen! The people at the Meadowlands complex, which includes Giants Stadium, were extremely nice to us. They said that it was only fitting for us to end our World Cup experience where we had started.

Bruce rocked the sold-out crowd and we danced for three hours straight. After the show, our back-up goalkeeper Saskia Webber, who is from New Jersey just like Bruce, somehow got backstage and gave him her U.S. team warm-up jacket. Bruce gave her his harmonica.

The next day *Sports Illustrated for Women* had a very nice function for us. It was a classy event. We got introduced one-by-one and paraded into a big room. There were about a dozen of us in directors' chairs onstage. They showed a great highlights video of the tournament and we answered questions for about a half hour in front of a couple hundred *Sports Illustrated* employees and sports businesspeople from New York. You could feel the warmth in the room and how proud of us everyone was. We got a huge ovation and once again were in awe of the effect we had on people. Then, we were finally done.

How did we feel after a week had passed and it had all sunk in? Relief? Pride? Exhaustion? Probably all of the above and more. One of the great things about our post-victory barnstorm was that once the games were over and we did all that media stuff, we got to relive everything. Several days after the Final, people were asking us what we were thinking during the game and the penalty kicks and the celebration. I wanted to say, "I don't even know. I haven't gotten enough sleep to even think about it." But, of course, I had thought about it, and after I talked to my teammates and our coaches and our fans, and all the media, it was then that I realized I had experienced the most incredible three weeks anyone can hope for.

I still look at the summer of '99 the same way. We are the pioneers of our sport and we have helped move women's soccer to a level of popularity never thought possible. We know we have a responsibility to ensure that legacy.

Winning is important, but the way we win is even more important. We want to play with a style and grace that encourages people to want to see our games. We want fans to realize the beauty of the sport, and to share our passion for it.

Is that why the country fell in love with us?

We all have our own theories. I hope it's the way we play, the way we interact with each other on and off the field, and the way we treat the people who come to watch us. They saw that we truly love what we do and that we gave everything we had to each other and to each game. They saw the spirit, emotion, unpredictability, and excitement that we generated. Most important, they saw us as a team.

To watch Briana make a save, or Michelle put her body on the line, or Joy swoop in to cut off another attack is to see us working for each other. When Brandi scored that tying goal against Germany, you could almost see the tremendous weight fly off her shoulders because she had rescued the team. People can relate to us. The little girls looked down at the field and saw themselves. We were them. They were us. We won together.

Talk the Talk

A Soccer Glossary

assist—The pass that leads to the goal. Many say it's as important as the goal itself, some say it's even more important.

attacking third—The part of the field loosely defined as the space from thirty-five yards out to your opponent's goal line. This is where you want the ball to be most of the game.

bend the ball—Impart spin on the ball with the inside or outside of your foot so that it dips and swerves around a defender or goalkeeper. Sometimes called a banana kick.

bicycle kick—The overhead kick made famous by Pelé, in which you throw your non-kicking leg in the air while simultaneously jumping and falling backwards, and then whip your kicking foot into the ball so you are striking it over your head as you fall softly (you hope) to the ground and cushion yourself with your hands. Not recommended for beginners or hard fields.

caps—Every time you play in an international match for your country, you are credited with a cap. You get a cap even if you only play one minute of the game. The term originates from the "olden" days when players received an actual knit cap (the kind you wear on your head) for each game played. Kristine Lilly has more caps than any man or woman in the history of soccer.

checking run—A run usually made by a center midfielder or a forward when she explodes back to the ball (away from the offensive third) in an effort create space between her and the defender.

cherry pick—Hang around the goal and wait for the ball to come to you for an easy shot. While you're waiting, you might as well be picking cherries, 'cause you aren't doing anything else. Sometimes it has a negative connotation, because you're not running if you're cherry picking, but a goal is a goal.

cover—Back up your fellow defender, so if she gets beat, you're in position to slow down the attacker or win the ball yourself.

cross—Pass the ball from the wings into the middle of the penalty box, whether on the ground or in the air. You want to do this as many times as possible in a game.

dead ball—You do not find this on the side of the freeway. It occurs when the game has stopped due to a foul and then is restarted from the spot of the infraction. Great teams take advantage of dead ball situations to score goals.

defensive third—The part of the field loosely defined as the space from your goal line to thirty-five yards out. This is where you don't want the ball to be.

dummy—Fake as if you're going to trap the ball or kick it, but instead let it roll between your legs or by you and (ideally) on to a teammate. This can make your opponent look foolish—thus the name.

far post—The goal post farther away from where you are crossing or shooting.

Féderation Internationale de Football Association (FIFA)—FIFA is the world governing body of soccer and the most powerful sports organization in the world. With a great deal of help from the local organizing committees in host countries, FIFA stages all the world championships for soccer, including the Women's World Cup.

50/50 ball—A loose ball that can be won by either team. Whoever wins the most often wins the match.

flat-back four—When the defense plays four defenders roughly in a line. All four have to be in sync for this defense to be effective. The flat-back four is an alternative to a stopper/sweeper formation where one defender plays deep behind the other three.

flick-on—A subtle touch of the ball with either your head or foot to guide it farther on its path or change its direction slightly.

garbage goal—This is not when you use two garbage cans for a makeshift goal, although you see that a lot. It is a sloppy goal that sometimes comes from a ball bouncing around inside the penalty box or hitting a defender and popping loose for an easy shot. This is not the prettiest way to score, but they all count the same.

ginga—A Brazilian term for the ability to dance, juke, and use all parts of your body to dribble past defenders, sometimes faking so much with your body that you don't need to touch the ball.

goalie box—The 6 × 20-yard lined area around the goal, inside the *penalty box*. The goalkeeper uses it to gauge where she is in relation to the goal at all times.

golden goal—Under a relatively new rule for FIFA championships, it is the first goal in sudden-death overtime, giving the scoring team the victory.

hat—Pop the ball over someone's head and collect it on the other side. Difficult to pull off, this can be really embarrassing to your opponent, even more so than a nutmeg. Not to be confused with a cap.

high pressure defense—A style of defense where you chase and put pressure on the other team all over the field, no matter who has the ball. Soccer's answer to the full-court press.

hold your run—Time your run so you won't be offside or perhaps arrive early for a pass.

hospital ball—A pass hit with too little pace and/or poor accuracy. Your teammate who is forced to try to collect that sloppy pass can often be at the bad end of a hard tackle and might end up in the hospital.

keep your shape—Maintain positional discipline on defense so that you don't leave gaps for the other team to attack. If you have too many players forward, or too many on one side of the field, you have lost your shape.

low bridge—Undercut a player as she is jumping for a head ball and knock her legs out from under her. This is a foul.

low pressure defense—A conservative style where you pull your players back into your own half and force the other team to try to work the ball through your packed defense.

man-to-man marking—A style of defense where players are assigned specific opponents to guard and are responsible for them all over the field.

mark—Do not, I repeat, do not draw on your opponent. Marking is soccer-speak for guarding.

near post—The post closer to where you are crossing or shooting. The goalkeeper should always have this post covered, but take a look—sometimes you can sneak the ball in there.

numbers up—Occurs when you have more players than the opponent in the attacking or defensive third. You always want to be numbers up on both ends of the field. That's why you have to do a lot of running in soccer.

nutmeg—Dribble the ball through an opponent's legs and collect it on the other side. Soccer's equivalent to an "in your face" slam dunk. Also the name of the official mascot for the 1999 FIFA Women's World Cup.

Olympic Development Program (ODP)—An identification system for elite players in the United States. Players can advance in the ODP from their district team to their state team to their regional team and, best of all, to the national team. Most of the players on the U.S. National Team played in the ODP, but certainly not all of them.

on—If a pass is "on," you should make it. If it is not "on," meaning that the space is too tight or there is a better option, you shouldn't.

on frame—Shooting the ball so it goes somewhere on the frame of the goal, whether it ends up being saved, pinging off the crossbar or post, or landing in the net.

overlapping run—When a player making the run overtakes her teammate with the ball. She can run inside or outside of her teammate, and it usually happens on the flanks.

own goal—Ouch! Everyone has done it. It's kicking or deflecting a ball into your own net. It happens, but just forget about it and try to get one back at the other end.

penalty box—The 18 × 44-yard lined area around the goal that should be ruled by the goalkeeper. It's the only area on the field in which the goalkeeper can touch the ball with her hands. If she ventures outside the box, she is under the same rules as a field player.

penalty kick (PK)—The referee awards this twelve-yard-spot kick when an attacker is fouled in the penalty box. Everyone except the kicker and the goalkeeper must be outside the box. Kickers should make nine out of ten, but somehow it always seems like they make fewer.

playing up—Playing for a team above your age level. It can be very valuable for a fourteen-year old to play with under-sixteens, or a seventeen-year-old to play for a women's team, but make sure you are being challenged and not overwhelmed. If you're spending a lot of time on the bench, you should play in your own age group.

rainbow—When you flick the ball over your own head (and sometimes the defender's) and trap it on the other side. This is often done with your heel and is very difficult to pull off in a game.

red card—You don't want one of these. If a referee shows you the red card, you are done for the day. Also known as

ejected, tossed, or sent off. It can also come with a sus-
pension of an additional game or more.

roof a shot—To hit a rocket that flies just under the crossbar and into the net.

scissors kick—Sounds like a professional wrestling move
and looks like a bicycle kick, except you fly through the
air and kick the ball with the side of your body parallel
to ground. You still thrust your non-kicking leg into the
air to get height and power and whip your kicking leg
through the ball.

second ball—A ball that pops loose after a head battle or a
50/50 tackle. You have to win the first ball *and* the second ball in order to be successful. It does no good to
win the header and then have the opponent win the
loose ball afterwards.

serve—To deliver pass, usually with a good deal of accuracy, to an attacker in scoring position. Nothing to do
with tennis, serving is setting the table for your teammates to feast.

serve a ball over the top—To hit a long pass over the
defense for your forwards to run onto.

shade—To force an attacker in a particular direction by
how you position your body. You want to shade her in
the direction in which you have the most support, which
is usually toward the sideline, the defenders best friend.

shielding—Keeping yourself between the ball and the
defender. It is a skill you must master to maintain possession in a game.

show someone your jersey number—To beat someone so
badly on the dribble that she is looking at your jersey
number as you run past her.

side-on position—Standing next to your opponent instead of behind her when you are marking her. This can help you get to the ball and win it, but be careful, it's easy to get burned if she has a quick first step.

skin a defender—Juke a defender so hard that you fake her right out of her skin. It also means to brush past an opponent on the run.

slide tackle—When you leave your feet and slide on the ground to win a ball. There is nothing like a good, hard slide tackle in a game to show your opponent who is in charge. But don't slide late, from behind or with your cleats up! (See: Red and Yellow Card).

slot your shot—To hit the ball hard, usually on the ground, and tuck it right into the corner of the goal in the side netting.

square—Not your math teacher. This is a pass made to a player who is directly to the side of you as opposed to a forward or back pass.

squared up—This is not wearing the same clothes as your math teacher. This is angling your body so you are in good position to receive the ball, most likely having your shoulders "square" or perpendicular to the approaching ball.

stoppage time—The time the referee adds to the 90 minutes. Often called injury time, this is a misnomer, as the referee can add minutes for other "stoppages" as well: when someone is given a yellow or red card, when the ball is out of bounds for an inordinate amount of time, and when debris (usually cups, coins, and t.p. hurled by rowdy fans) needs to be cleared off the field.

stopper—The defender that plays in front of the sweeper

and most likely is charged with marking one of the center forwards.

sudden-death overtime—An extra period where the first goal means victory to the team that scored it. Almost all international tournaments feature sudden-death overtime nowadays. *See also* **golden goal**.

sweeper—The last player in the defense besides the goalkeeper, she patrols behind the other defenders and is responsible for "sweeping" away all the loose balls that get past her teammates.

switch fields—To pass the ball from one side of the field to the other, in one or two passes. By quickly changing the angle of attack, you can confuse the defense and take advantage of openings that will inevitably appear as the defenders scramble to adjust.

thru ball—To play a pass behind the defense for one of your players to run onto. This pass has to be made with perfect pace and accuracy so it beats the defense and allows attackers to collect it before the goalkeeper.

touchline—The touchline is the sideline. If you hear an English soccer announcer say that the ball "goes into touch" it just means that it is out of bounds.

U.S. Soccer Federation or **U.S. Soccer**—This is the organization that governs soccer in the United States and organizes the national teams, from U16 (under sixteen years old) to the Women's National Team.

USA mentality—The attitude that fuels the U.S. Women's National Team, it says we will never stop fighting to win on the field, for each other and for ourselves.

weak side—This is the side of the field where the ball is not. Players tend to migrate to the ball, which means the weak side will often have fewer defenders and more room to maneuver. *See also* **switch fields**.

weight—The proper pace on a pass so your teammate can trap it easily and be productive.

width—Using the wide players on the field to spread out a defense. A good team must use width to create options in the middle, because that's where the goal is.

wind-up—Pulling your leg back as if to shoot or pass, but then dribbling instead. A very effective fake, especially if you set it up by blasting the ball at a defender's leg in the beginning of the game.

work rate—A gauge of how much a player is running and helping her team in a game. You want to have a high work rate.

World Cup—The ultimate goal for a soccer player is to win the World Cup. The tournament is held every four years and, by virtue of a two-year-long exhaustive qualifying round, features the best teams in the world.

yellow card—If you get one of these, it is just a warning, but if you get two of them, you will also see a red card and be ejected. Also called a caution. You can get a yellow card for many things, but usually it is for committing a hard or dangerous foul, arguing with the referee, or using unsportsmanlike language.

zone defense—A style of defense in which the defenders stay in their zones and mark the players that come into their areas. This, like all defense, necessitates good communication among teammates.

Photography Credits

Page 168: Al Bello/Allsport; Page 115: Simon Bruty; Page 141: Ezra Chan; Page 121: Jonathan Daniel/Allsport; Pages 13, 65: *Durham Herald-Sun*, Durham, N.C.; Pages 68, 69, 70, 71, 98, 99, 123, 128, 129, 137, 139, 153, 172, 173: Jay Farbman; Pages 17, 44, 108, 109, 110, 111, 146: Dean Forbes/Sportstock; Pages 4, 29, 39: Stephanie Hamm; Pages 100, 190: Andy Lyons/Allsport; Page 26: Nike, Inc.; Page 62: PAM/ISI; Page 207: Neil Rittenbury; Pages 20, 33, 37, 50, 82, 86, 119, 125, 127, 150, 155, 179, 198, 209, 210: Phil Stephens Photography; Pages 53, 73, 162, 163, 171, 89, 143, 181, 185, 193, 197, 203: J. Brett Whitesell/ISI

Insert 1: Pages 4, 5, 6 (top), 7 (top): *Durham Herald-Sun*, Durham, N.C.; Pages 1, 2, 7 (bottom): Stephanie Hamm; Page 8 (top): Michael Stahlschmidt/Sideline Sports Photography; Page 3: Phil Stephens Photography; Pages 6 (bottom), 8 (bottom): J. Brett Whitesell/ISI

Insert 2: Page 6 (top): Dean Forbes/Sportstock; Page 1 (top): Andy Lyons/Allsport; Pages 2, 4 (bottom): Michael Stahlschmidt/Sideline Sports Photography; Pages 1 (bottom), 3, 4 (top left and right), 5, 6 (bottom): Phil Stephens Photography; Page 8: Rick Stewart/Allsport; Page 7: Brett Whitesell, ISI.